The Biblical Foundations of the Doctrine of Justification

The Biblical Foundations of the Doctrine of Justification

An Ecumenical Follow-Up to the *Joint Declaration on the Doctrine of Justification*

*Presented by a task force
of biblical scholars and systematic theologians from
the Lutheran World Federation,
the Pontifical Council for Promoting Christian Unity,
the World Communion of Reformed Churches,
and the World Methodist Council*

Paulist Press
New York / Mahwah, New Jersey

The Scripture quotations contained herein are from the New Revised Standard Version: Catholic Edition, Copyright © 1989 and 1993, by the Division of Christian Education of the National Council of the Churches of Christ in the United States of America. Used by permission. All rights reserved.

Cover design by Cristina Cancel
Book design by The HK Scriptorium

Copyright © 2012 by Lutheran World Federation and the Pontifical Council for Promoting Christian Unity
All rights reserved. No part of this book may be reproduced or transmitted in any form or by any means, electronic or mechanical, including photocopying, recording or by any information storage and retrieval system without permission in writing from the Publisher.

Library of Congress Control Number: 2012936577

Published by Paulist Press
997 Macarthur Boulevard
Mahwah, New Jersey 07430

www.paulistpress.com

Printed and bound in the United States of America

In Memoriam

Rev. Dr. Lawrence Boadt, CSP
1942–2010
Member of the Task Force, 2008-2010

Contents

Preface ix

Foreword xiii

I. Introduction 1

II. Hermeneutical Aspects 7

III. Traditions of Biblical Interpretation 15

IV. The Old Testament 27

V. The New Testament 57

VI. The Bible and the *JDDJ*—Conclusion 107

Notes 113

Members of the Task Force 117

Scripture Index 119

Preface

This is a book full of promise.

Written to honor a pledge of continued conversation between two partners, it became the common project of an expanded circle and now itself offers a promise to ecumenical contexts around the world: come and see—come and develop!—the insights that appear through attentive reading, listening, and discussing together the central affirmations of our faith, based on their biblical foundations.

This study fulfills a commitment made on 31 October 1999, when representatives of the Catholic Church and the Lutheran World Federation met in Augsburg, Germany, for the signing of the historic *Joint Declaration on the Doctrine of Justification.*

With that act, the churches declared that it was no longer necessary to repeat the centuries-old mutual condemnations on the crucial subject of justification. Walter Cardinal Kasper, then Secretary of the Pontifical Council for Promoting Christian Unity and one of the signers, looked back on that moment from his later position as President of the Pontifical Council: "We held out our hands to each other as churches and we do not wish to let go ever again" (Walter Kasper, *That They All May Be One: The Call to Unity* [New York: Continuum, 2004], 127).

But it was clear, even in that moment of joy and accomplishment, that work remained to be done. Recognizing this, the "Official Common Statement" for the signing of the *JDDJ* (para. 3) declared, "The two partners in dialogue are committed to continued and deepened study of the biblical foundations of the doctrine of justification." Other topics concerning justification were identified also, but "biblical foundations" was the first.

It was evident also that the hands joined together in Augsburg needed to reach out to a wider circle of participants. There were other church families with a stake and a voice in this discussion. The Reformed had participated fully in the history of theological debates concerning justification, and so their inclusion was rightly deemed indispensable. The Methodists came by a different path. When in 2006 the World Methodist Council affirmed the *Joint Declaration*, a church family that had not shared in the sixteenth-century quarrels found in the *Declaration* a statement of their own faith. It thus became essential that Methodist scholars also were included in this project. In this way the task force became a quadrilateral one, with representatives not only of the Pontifical Council for Promoting Christian Unity and the Lutheran World Federation but also from the World Alliance of Reformed Churches (since 2010 the World Communion of Reformed Churches) and from the World Methodist Council.

Composition of the taskforce was not the only question to be answered. It was a challenging task to shape the questions and to find a means of consultative writing that would be appropriate for specialists in both Old and New Testament, for biblical scholars together with theologians. Bishop emeritus Dr. Walter Klaiber, for whose experienced leadership we are very grateful, describes this process in the Foreword.

Now we can celebrate that this book is before us for reading and for common study. It is a deep pleasure to each of us to see the work, promised for more than a decade, brought to completion. The biblical foundations of the doctrine of justification have indeed been explored more deeply! For this work, we express our warm thanks to all members of the task force.

This book turns out to be the fulfillment of promise in another way, a way that is finally more significant. In establishing this task force, we trusted that collaborative study of biblical texts could offer a promising way forward toward ecumenically accountable appreciations of the doctrine of justification—and this hope has been richly vindicated. Careful reading of this book reveals many ways, small and large, in which the task force's distinctive combination of perspectives and methods brought fresh insights to the reading of the Bible—and in turn, the interpretation of Scripture casts aspects of the theology of justification into new light. In attending carefully to one another's readings, members of the task force discovered that their interpretations were no longer a reason for church division. At the same time, bringing the texts into conversation with ongoing ecumenical discussions provided a helpful lens for theologians and exegetes alike.

We believe that this book invites the attention of a wide audience. It is not written only for biblical scholars, or principally for theologians, although specialists in these disciplines will find much to reward them here. The questions and needs of the church were always before the task force, and they have provided here a text that is accessible to many attentive readers who care about Christian confession of God's grace and about the unity of the church.

In this book, we find fulfillment of a promise made in the last century, and the promise offered of wisdom yet to come in the common exploration of our faith. Take it and read!

>
> Rev. Martin Junge
> General Secretary
> Lutheran World Federation
>
> Rev. Dr. Setri Nyomi
> General Secretary
> World Communion of Reformed Churches
>
> Bishop Dr. Brian Farrell
> Secretary
> Pontifical Council for Promoting
> Christian Unity
>
> Rev. Dr. George H. Freeman
> General Secretary
> World Methodist Council

Foreword

From the first session of the symposium of biblical scholars, held at the highly symbolic site of San Paolo fuori le mure in Rome in October 2008, we found ourselves in an ambiguous situation. We were a group of four Old Testament and six New Testament scholars plus two systematic theologians, coming from four continents and representing the Catholic, Lutheran, Methodist, and Reformed theological traditions. We had been called together to fulfill the commitment made by the signing partners of the *Joint Declaration on the Doctrine of Justification (JDDJ)* in the "Official Common Statement," 3: "to continued and deepened study of the biblical foundations of the doctrine of justification." But this task force needed to take account of two different aspects. On the one hand, the *JDDJ* would not have been possible had not the biblical scholarship of the last century prepared the ground for a common understanding of Paul's doctrine of justification and of its Old Testament foundations. On the other, over the last two or three decades this consensus had been challenged by new perspectives emerging from the studies of Paul's theology that have called into question the whole approach of Western theology to Paul's doctrine of justification, in Roman Catholic and the Reformation tradition alike.

Nonetheless, the group was all the more convinced that a concise study of the biblical foundations of the doctrine of justification would be helpful—not only in light of the continuing ecumenical dialogue on this issue but also with regard to how to preach and teach the message of justification for people today. With this in mind, the group decided to continue its work and to produce the requested study. The leading principles and the short history of this process are described in the Introduction. The respective chapters of the study were drafted by different members of the group and then discussed and revised, first by the colleagues in the same field and finally by the whole group. Thus, there may still be a few inconsistencies in the text, but, in principle, the whole group takes responsibility for the entire study. We see the results of our work as a study document that may stimulate further discussion, both through the consensus it presents and also through the remnants of some tensions it does not seek to conceal.

We hand this study over to its mandating bodies, the Lutheran World Federation, the Pontifical Council for Promoting Christian Unity, the World Communion of Reformed Churches and the World Methodist Council, with the hope that it will help to deepen our common understanding of the biblical message of justification and thereby to foster our joint efforts to share the gospel of Jesus Christ with the people of our time.

We are thankful to those who have entrusted us with this task for the opportunity to work together, and especially to the staff of the LWF for their support in editing this text.

We deeply mourn our colleague, Rev. Dr. Lawrence Boadt, CSP, who died of cancer shortly after our meeting in Louisville. He was a wonderful colleague with great theological competence, very warm and friendly, with a good sense of humor, and a strong faith in and love of God. May he rest in peace and see what he believed! We dedicate this book to his memory.

We are very grateful to Paulist Press and its president, the Reverend Doctor Mark-David Janus, CSP, for making it possible for this ecumenical study to be published. Publication of the study is a wonderful tribute to the memory of the Reverend Doctor Lawrence Boadt, CSP, who served as a member of the task force until his much-regretted death in the spring of 2010. Last but not least, we want to thank the Reverend Doctor Raymond Collins, who, as a member of the task force, took on the burden of reading the proofs and preparing the index; we thank as well Dr. Maurya Horgan of the Scriptorium for her careful copyediting, and Donna Crilly and Diane Flynn of Paulist Press who guided this work to its completion.

On behalf of the task force,

Bishop emeritus Walter F. Klaiber

I

Introduction

The *Joint Declaration on the Doctrine of Justification*

On 31 October 1999, representatives of the Lutheran World Federation (LWF) and the Roman Catholic Church solemnly signed the *Joint Declaration on the Doctrine of Justification*[1] in Augsburg, Germany, by putting their signatures on the "Official Common Statement." The statement ends with the words: "By this act of signing The Catholic Church and The Lutheran World Federation confirm the Joint Declaration on the Doctrine of Justification in its entirety." The words "in its entirety" mean that both signing partners affirm the two results of the *Declaration*:

> The understanding of the doctrine of justification set forth in this *Declaration* shows that a consensus in basic truths of the doctrine of justification exists between Lutherans and Catholics. In light of this consensus the remaining differences of language, theological elaboration, and emphasis in the understanding of justification described in paras. 18 to 39 are acceptable. Therefore the Lutheran and the Catholic explications of justification are in their difference open to one another and do not destroy the consensus regarding the basic truths.
>
> Thus the doctrinal condemnations of the sixteenth century, insofar as they relate to the doctrine of justification, appear in a new light: The teaching of the Lutheran churches presented in this *Declaration* does not fall under the condemnations of the Council of Trent. The condemnations in the Lutheran Confessions do not apply to the teaching of the Roman Catholic Church presented in this *Declaration*.[3]

Both results belong together. It would not make any sense to claim a consensus regarding the doctrine of justification if certain condemnations were still to apply to the other church's teaching. And the other way round: without stating the consensus achieved, which explains what both sides have in common in spite of remaining differences, it would be impossible to declare that the condemnations do not apply.[4] The concept of consensus implicit in the *JDDJ* ("differentiated consensus" or "differentiating consensus") does not exclude differences; rather, it integrates explicitly certain differences with the claim that they are not church dividing.

The *JDDJ* is an official document of the Catholic Church and the LWF. Thus, its status is quite different from the status of the results of bilateral dialogue groups. The latter represent only the opinions of theologians involved in these dialogues, even if they have received a mandate from their respective churches. Thus, the *JDDJ* represents a new level of ecumenical relations, since it expresses the official position of the churches involved.

This short text claims to overcome a deep controversy that has lasted for more than four centuries. It is based on over forty years of theological work carried out by many individual scholars and such national dialogues as the U.S. dialogue "Justification by Faith,"[5] Germany's "Lehrverurteilungen—kirchentrennend?" ["The Condemnations of the Reformation Era. Do They Still Divide?"],[6] and the international Catholic–Lutheran dialogue, for example, the "Malta-Document" (no. 26), which already in 1972 stated, "Today, however, a far-reaching consensus is developing in the interpretation of justification."[7] The Lutheran–Roman Catholic document "Church and Justification" elaborates on the relationship between the doctrine of justification and the doctrine of the church.[8]

The *JDDJ* presents the main, basic results of that dialogue to the Catholic Church and the Lutheran churches in a short text, asking them whether they see their own respective doctrine represented in the document and whether they can agree with the two main results referred to above. In affirming the *JDDJ* in the course of 1999, after a very intense discussion, both churches performed a doctrinal act. They did not do so separately, but jointly. Due to the complex process of reception and decision making, a so-called Annex was added that affirmed the results of the *JDDJ* and safeguarded them against misunderstandings.

The authority of the *JDDJ* rests on both the doctrinal act that the churches performed by signing the *JDDJ* and the theological work that lies behind it. Thus, some of the studies and dialogues on which the *JDDJ* draws are explicitly mentioned in an appendix called "Sources for the *JDDJ*."[9] This background material has, of course, not the same doctrinal authority as the *JDDJ* itself, but in order to follow the arguments that support the statements of this document one also has to study that material.

Following the signing of the *JDDJ* and, after a long process of careful reflection and discussion within the Methodist churches, the latter expressed a wish to associate with the *JDDJ*. The signing partners invited and welcomed the Methodists to reflect on joining the *JDDJ*. Since the Methodists were not involved in the sixteenth-century conflicts between Lutherans and Catholics, they could not simply sign the *JDDJ*. Instead, a Statement of Association was drafted, in which

Methodists explain their respective emphases in understanding justification, just as Catholics and Lutherans do in chapter 4 of the *JDDJ*, and Methodists declare that their understanding is in consonance with the respective parts of the *JDDJ*. Lutherans and Catholics welcomed this explanation, thus declaring that they were in agreement with it.[10] On 23 July 2006, Methodist, Catholic, and Lutheran representatives solemnly signed this Statement in Seoul.

The Exegetical Section of the *JDDJ*: "Biblical Message of Justification" and the Critique Thereof

Paragraph 8 of the *JDDJ* begins with the sentence: "Our common way of listening to the word of God in Scripture has led to such new insights." This refers to the previous paragraph, which reads, "Developments have taken place that not only make possible but also require the churches to examine the divisive questions and condemnations and see them in a new light."[11] Thereby an important role in the ecumenical rapprochement is attributed to modern exegesis. While this sentence invited high expectations of this section, the very limited space for the exegetical section did not allow for elaborating exegetical insights and arguments in any detail. The original text of this section (*JDDJ*, 8-12), drafted by John Reumann and Joseph Fitzmyer,[12] focused on the use of New Testament language concerning gospel, justification, and righteousness. In the revision meetings of the *JDDJ*, their text was significantly changed by taking up many of the proposals that had been presented by the churches.

In the public debate on the *JDDJ*, various criticisms have been made:

- The biblical quotations are not interpreted within the textual and historical contexts from which they are taken; rather, they are more or less used as isolated propositions and the biblical quotations are organized mainly according to dogmatic perspectives.
- The Pauline statements on justification are, contrary to Paul's own usage, not related to the Christ event and the gospel of the death and resurrection of Jesus Christ.
- Other New Testament texts that deal with God's righteousness (mainly in Matthew and James) are not sufficiently taken into consideration.
- The text is too focused on those biblical verses in which the words "just," "justify," "justification," and "righteousness" occur, but the Bible expresses salvation in other terms, too. Thus, certain important references for this topic are not mentioned.
- The reference the text makes to the Old Testament is one-sided: important Old Testament passages that express God's righteousness are missing; the

biblical witness to God and God's saving action for creation and the people of Israel is almost totally missing, and there is an inadequate view of the law in the Old Testament.
- New insights into the early Jewish context and the genesis of Pauline theology do not play a role in the text (e.g., the missionary situation of Paul, the relationship between Israel and the church).

Nevertheless, it should be appreciated that the *JDDJ* begins with a section on the "Biblical Message of Justification."

The Task Force's Mandate

Both Lutherans and Catholics felt that these critical observations should be taken seriously, and that joint future work on the exegetical problems of the doctrine of justification should benefit from this critique. Thus, they stated in the "Official Common Statement," "The two partners in dialogue are committed to continued and deepened study of the biblical foundations of the doctrine of justification."[13] In order to fulfill this commitment, a small group of Lutheran and Roman Catholic exegetes met in Rome in 2006 (12–14 March) and developed a plan for a task force to be presented to the Lutheran World Federation and the Pontifical Council for Promoting Christian Unity (PCPCU). Since the Methodists declared their agreement with the *JDDJ* in 2006, it was clear that Methodist exegetes should participate in the work of this group too. Reformed theologians were also invited, since the World Alliance of Reformed Churches (WARC) had reflected on their relationship to the *JDDJ*. It was proposed that Old Testament scholars and two systematic theologians should be part of the group in order to integrate the Old Testament witness and keep systematic perspectives in mind.

The group was established with the approval of the four mandating bodies (LWF, PCPCU, WARC [now the World Communion of Reformed Churches], and the World Methodist Council). It met in Rome, at the Benedictine Abbey of St. Paul Outside the Walls, 2–5 October 2008; at the Louisville Presbyterian Theological Seminary, Louisville, Kentucky, 13–17 January 2010; and in Germany at the Colleg Wittenberg, Wittenberg, 4–7 February 2011.

The task force identified the following tasks and challenges:

- Not to start from the controversies of the sixteenth century but to interpret the biblical texts in their own context, with their own constructs, concepts, and emphases. The multiplicity of approaches in the Bible should be presented while seeking their unity. Thus this study does not seek to comment on the exegetical section of the *JDDJ*.
- To take seriously that New Testament texts constantly refer to the Christ event, of which the apostolic gospel is the witness, expressed in different

Introduction

forms (narratives, short creedal formulas, theological reflection) and with different concepts and styles.
- To integrate new insights in Pauline research into the study: the new evaluation of early Judaism (pre-Rabbinic Judaism, Qumran, Jewish-Hellenistic literature), the new evaluation of the Torah (as opposed to the negative evaluation of the law in some parts of Lutheranism, though not in Luther), a new perspective on Israel, the genesis of the Pauline theology of justification in the context of mission, and different perspectives of several Pauline letters.
- To be challenged by insights and achievements of the Jewish–Christian dialogue. The doctrine of justification cannot be developed without a theology of Israel, whereas Israel and the place of the Old Testament in the Christian Bible cannot appropriately be understood without theological reflection on the relationship to the Christ event as explained in Paul.
- To develop inner-biblical relations: The concept of the "righteousness of God" shows relations between different books in the New Testament and the deep connections between certain Old Testament traditions and the New Testament. The study has to elaborate on the relationship between the concepts of "righteousness of God" and "kingdom of God"—the center of Jesus' proclamation.
- To keep in mind the hermeneutical problems of Scripture and tradition, of the history of scriptural exegesis and the significance of exegetical findings for a systematic treatment of the respective problems, even though the study is basically meant to be an exegetical one.

The German dialogue document, *The Condemnations of the Reformation Era—Do They Still Divide?* contains an introductory chapter explaining the method of overcoming doctrinal controversies. The section entitled "The Authority of Holy Scripture and Its Interpretation as Foundation for an Understanding of the Beliefs Disputed in the Mutual Condemnations"[14] claims, "Today it is possible to say the following: Far-reaching agreement in the interpretation of Holy Scripture"[15] significantly contributed to reaching a mutual understanding. The task force has tried to substantiate this claim.

II

Hermeneutical Aspects

This study intends to investigate the biblical foundations of the doctrine of justification. This presupposes hermeneutical reflections on different topics:

- It is the aim of this study to refer the Christian doctrine of justification to the witness of the Old Testament. This may not be done without some considerations on the relationship between the Old and New Testaments.
- It is necessary to determine the place of Scripture with regard to revelation, which is not identical with Scripture but finds its basic and normative witness in Scripture.
- Regarding this witness, it has to be recognized that it includes a diversity of expressions converging in their testimony to God's salvific action toward human beings while at the same time choosing diverse accents in order to correspond to diverse situations.
- Being aware that controversies and ecumenical efforts frequently concern doctrinal and existential traditions, even a biblical study has to deal with this horizon by reflecting on the relationship of Scripture and tradition(s) as well as by drawing attention to the question of how Scripture may be the yardstick for traditions concerning justification.
- One aspect of this comparison between Scripture and traditions is awareness of traditional interpretations of Scripture. Chapter III will give some examples of traditions of biblical interpretation and provide hermeneutical reflections concerning the comparison of former and contemporary exegesis.

1. Definitions

Points of convergence in the present understanding of revelation, Scripture, and tradition in ecumenical dialogues can be summarized with three terms that form the basis for mutually acceptable hermeneutical guidelines:

- Revelation refers to God's salvific action toward creation, the people of Israel, and all people as principally witnessed to in the Old and New Testaments.
- Scripture is the authoritative witness of God's revelation. This witness is inspired by the Holy Spirit, framed in human words and entrusted to the church to be handed down to all humanity.
- Tradition is the process of handing down the witness of revelation in and through the church. Tradition is subject to the authority of Scripture and is measured according to it. Guided by the Holy Spirit, tradition unfolds in the church as a living process of transmission in specific, concrete traditions, that is, doctrinal and existential traditions.

On the basis of these definitions, the following principles can be formulated for discussing and reflecting hermeneutically on the witness to revelation, Holy Scripture, and the sacred tradition in the church:

- The testimony of God's saving revelation is fundamentally brought up in Scripture and actualized by the tradition of the church.
- The tradition of the church today has to be measured according to Scripture's testimony to revelation.
- The testimony of Scripture reveals God's saving acts and brings up these events today with the help of church tradition.

Church tradition is necessary to safeguard the contemporary relevance of revelation. Scripture is necessary to safeguard the authenticity of the tradition of the church. Together Scripture and tradition pave the way for the encounter with God's revelation in Jesus Christ today.

2. The Relationship between the Old and New Testaments

The emergence of the church's biblical canon is deeply rooted in and theologically linked to the Jewish Scriptures. "Scripture(s)" (*graphē/graphai*) in the New Testament always refers to the Jewish Scriptures, although, historically, the formation of the canon of the church took place in parallel with the delimitation and consolidation of the "Hebrew Bible" in early Rabbinic Judaism. For the church, the canonical biblical witness does not exist without the Old Testament. The theological basis for this resides in the Christian understanding of God.

Regarding the witness of the Old Testament to the theology of justification, a hermeneutical appreciation of the relationship between the two testaments is needed. In the context of Christian belief, the theological appreciation thereof takes the New Testament as its point of departure.

The church owes its existence to the "calling" action of the one God of Israel as witnessed in the Old Testament, who, according to the New Testament, is confessed as the Father of Jesus Christ. Jesus, according to the testimony of Scripture, is believed to be "Immanuel," as "God with us" (Isa 7:14; Matt 1:22–24), who, as the risen Lord, promises to his disciples, "I am with you always, to the end of the age" (cf. Matt 28:18–20). He is the one who pours out the promised Holy Spirit from God's right hand (Acts 2:33).

Thus, from a Christian point of view, the Old Testament witness is especially relevant for the church since it can be understood as a witness of Christian faith on the basis of belief in the Triune God and, as such, is a constituent component of the biblical witness to God's revelation in Christ. This is the legitimate Christian claim to an interpretation of the Old Testament from a Christian perspective. On the other hand, Christians today have to honor a Jewish self-understanding that is based on the covenant between God and God's people Israel as witnessed in the biblical Scriptures.

The overall biblical witness can be ascertained only by placing the individual biblical texts in their canonical context and within the framework of the relationship between Old and New Testaments. This leads to two fundamental categories of biblical statements:

- The common witness to revelation of both testaments consists in their proclamation of the salvific action of the one God of the entire Bible toward God's people, humankind, and all creation.
- The specific witness to revelation of the New Testament consists in its proclamation of the Christ event as the eschatological accomplishment of God's salvific action toward the church and the world.

With regard to the understanding of God, there is fundamental concurrence in both testaments of the Christian Bible: The one God of Israel is confessed as the Father of Jesus Christ (cf. 1 Cor 8:6). Salvation can come only from God. Humanity, meanwhile, is capable of destroying its relationship to God, but not of establishing or preserving it. Nevertheless, people are called to live according to God's will, to love their neighbors and to praise God as their creator and redeemer. This is a significant point of convergence in the Old and New Testaments' understandings of the relationship between God and humanity. Therefore, also by reading the Old Testament, Christians can become acquainted with the Triune God, who is not dissuaded by human disobedience from bringing God's salvific purpose to fruition or from creating a fellowship precisely there where humanity becomes aware it is not possible to do so and even attempts to prevent it (cf. Hos 11:8–9).

The Old Testament witnesses to God's salvific actions toward the people of Israel; the New Testament, to God's eschatological action toward Israel and all humankind in Jesus Christ. Whereas in the Old Testament God's dealing with the peoples of the world is subordinated to God's action toward Israel, in the New

Testament Jews and Gentiles together are beneficiaries of God's grace. Hence, the link between the two testaments may be called salvation history (*Heilsgeschichte*). However, this must be understood as a theological affirmation, distinct from historically demonstrable continuities between the history of Israel and that of the church. From a theological perspective, the continuity between Israel and the church is based only on the action of the one God of Israel, who is confessed as the Father of Jesus Christ. Implicit in this belief is that, in Christ, God fulfills God's promise of salvation to Israel by calling Israel and all peoples to be the eschatological people of God (Rom 9:22–24).

The writings of the New Testament already contain christological, eschatological, and ecclesiological interpretations of Old Testament texts, which, according to Christian belief, cannot be relinquished, because the Old Testament forms a constituent part of the Christian Bible. This does not preclude but rather ensures that the authentic and specific word of the Old Testament as the word of God may be listened to by the church. But, according to the Christian understanding, this word is still the word of the Triune God, who sealed and upholds God's covenant with Israel, whose Holy Spirit was at work in Jesus of Nazareth, and who in Christ called forth the church from Israel and all peoples and brings it to fulfillment.

3. The Relationship between the Christ Event and the Multiform Witness of Scripture

The Christ event as the content of apostolic witness precedes the New Testament Scriptures and the biblical canon. It has the quality of revelation and stands above the Christian faith and the church.

As its subject and prerequisite, the one and only Christ event precedes the multiform apostolic proclamation (*kērygma*), which is not identical to but yet is inseparable from the Christ event. The apostles received the Christ event in an exclusive encounter with the risen Christ, who entrusted them with the message of salvation. This is what accounts for the uniqueness, singularity, and irreversible end point of the one apostolic proclamation (cf. 1 Cor 15:8–9). To this extent, there is a categorical difference between the first apostolic proclamation as witnessed to in the New Testament and its various transmissions to the church, in the church, and by the church.

It is the one and same Christ event that is presented by various testimonies forming the one apostolic witness. Nevertheless, the Christ event can be made accessible only by means of the diversity of kerygmatic and didactic idioms. Therefore there is an inevitable hermeneutical circle.

The diverse expressions of the apostolic proclamation in the apostles' witness form the basis of the New Testament canon. The apostles' fellowship in their proclamation of the gospel, as shown exemplarily in the New Testament (cf. 1 Cor

15:1–11; Acts 15; Gal 2:1–10), can be understood as a canonical template for reading the Bible. From the perspective of the Christ event, the canon is genuinely valid only when its unity as well as the tension between its parts is preserved. Such unity and tension exist in the relationship between the one act of salvation, to which the church owes its existence, and the different testimonies to it in the texts of the New Testament.

According to the New Testament, the apostles, the first recipients of the revelation in Christ and normative witnesses to Christ, act in communion and agree on the core of their witness. They proclaim the message about Jesus' ministry, his salvific death on the cross, and his being raised from the dead by God. Their names are associated with the first proclamation of Christ as the origin of the church on earth. The historically multifaceted nature of the unique Christ event is thus symbolically enshrined in and entrusted to the canon of Scripture.

The gospel, which brought the church into existence, is also the criterion on which its fellowship is based. The one gospel was transmitted to the apostles in a single, unique, and definitive manner. The unity of the one gospel was to be retained, even in the face of disagreement or opposition (cf. Gal 2:11–14). According to the New Testament witness, the apostles remained in communion by their conciliar fellowship as the recipients of the gospel (cf. Gal 2:8–9). Because the gospel as the word of the one God can only be one and there can be no other (cf. Gal 1:6–9), only the apostolic fellowship can bear a credible witness to it.

The Pauline doctrine of justification is to be understood as one, but not the only, such kerygmatic and didactic formulation of the Christ event. It is not one and the same as the apostolic witness to Christ, but it partakes of it and has the same status as the other apostles' formulations of the Christ event. It is equal in terms of origin, content, authority, and normativity: "Whether then it was I or they, so we proclaim and so you have come to believe" (1 Cor 15:11).

To be sure, the apostolic proclamation, in all its forms, is the process of receiving and of transmitting a gift; both are the result of God's gift of grace. God's grace, in the sense of self-surrender for the sake of humanity, determines the content of the apostolic witness to Christ, as well as its transmission in the proclamation of Christ to all people.

In order to broaden the biblical basis of the doctrine of justification, we must look for such formulations of the proclamation of Christ in the New Testament. These are essentially homogeneous (in the sense of the apostolic witness to Christ), although the doctrinal reflection on and interpretations of them (in the sense of the tradition of the church) may differ with regard to what is emphasized. The most important sources in this regard are:

- The Letters of Paul (especially Romans and Galatians), which fundamentally develop and reflect the doctrine of justification in the face of compromising the proclamation of the gospel in Pauline churches.

- The Gospel of Matthew (cf. Matt 3:15; 5:6, 10, 20; 6:33) as a witness to the righteousness of God embodied in the Messiah, Jesus Christ, in his proclamation and realization of the lordship of God and in his call to his disciples to do justice.
- The Letter of James with its reference to the "harvest of righteousness" (cf. Jas 3:18) as a necessary consequence of the revelation of the "word of truth" (cf. Jas 1:18) and a constituent component of a living faith.

The criterion for evaluating and classifying these apostolic witnesses in the biblical message of justification is how well they correspond to the Christ event, to the gospel of Christ, and to the action, way, and destiny of Jesus of Nazareth, in whom God accomplished God's justification for the salvation of humanity.

4. Tradition as the Unfolding of Scripture and the Witness of Scripture as the Yardstick for Tradition

The necessity of tradition results from the universal relevance of justification itself. Since all people are called by God to salvation in Christ (cf. *JDDJ*, 16), and the message of justification as witnessed in Scripture should potentially reach all persons, tradition is necessary as the means of its transmission in different times and contexts. A living tradition of this kind already exists in the New Testament when the Pauline theology of justification is transposed from the framework of the mission to the Gentiles into other contexts (see, e.g., Ephesians 2).

This living tradition manifests itself in various traditions because faith in the justifying God finds concrete expression in doctrinal models and ways of living. We can consider this tradition as a pneumatically founded reality, which is a manner of adopting the biblical message. However, whereas the biblical canon identifies a multiplicity of witnesses to be definitively legitimate and normative, the various traditions deserve a critical examination in light of the witness of Scripture. Thus, Scripture is a sort of rule and standard for traditions and a point of orientation for the plurality of diverse articulations of faith.

The *JDDJ* brings out the difference between Scripture and its doctrinal transposition by differentiating between the message of justification and the doctrine of justification. By doing this it emphasizes the necessity to dissolve a too simple identification between the foundation of Christian faith and its doctrinal exposition, as well as—we may add here—its traditional expressions.

"Opposing interpretations and applications of the biblical message of justification were a principal point of the division of the Western church in the sixteenth century...."[1] For this reason, the *JDDJ* links the task of striving "to deepen this common understanding to that of making it bear fruit in the life and teaching of the churches."[2] It is therefore essential to relate reflection on the biblical foundations of the doctrine of justification to reflection on the scriptural soundness of verbal, doctrinal, and existential traditions that pertain to the message of justification and, if necessary, critically to examine them in the light of Scripture. However, evaluating conformity to Scripture is a task of juxtaposing exegetical questions and hermeneutical reflections as to how the biblical texts may play their role as a yardstick to measure confessional traditions.

An intermediate level springs to mind when relating Scripture and traditions, namely, traditions of interpreting Scripture. Once exegetical insights and specific interpretational traditions can be brought into dialogue with each other, then a deepening and broadening of the biblical basis of the doctrine of justification will occur. The use of biblical passages in classic Protestant and Catholic doctrinal statements on justification is to be explicitly discussed and clarified in the light of modern exegetical insights. The problems arising from this endeavor will be presented in the following chapter.

III

Traditions of Biblical Interpretation

The interpretations of biblical texts to be presented in this study underlie certain presuppositions, aims, and methods different from those used in the church for many centuries, including during the Reformation. This chapter considers examples of exegetical debates concerning Paul's Letter to the Romans that played a role in Reformation controversies. Although throughout earlier centuries theologians often distinguished between biblical commentaries and doctrinal works, in their debates exegetical and systematic aspects, as we would call them today, were deeply intertwined. Thus, it is difficult to relate findings of historical-critical research to this tradition of exegesis. Despite considerable internal diversity and developments in these commentaries over time, exegetical tasks were regarded very differently from how we comment on biblical texts today. Thus, a reflection on the problem of relating recent exegetical findings to traditional interpretations of Scripture and contemporary understandings of the Christian faith will conclude the chapter.

1. The Righteousness of God

Martin Luther's basic Reformation insight was focused on a new understanding of the expression "righteousness of God." The meaning of this formula is much debated in contemporary exegesis, which is often critical of Luther's understanding. Thus, it may be helpful to see what Luther had in mind and in which context he developed his understanding of this expression.

> But up till then it was not the cold blood about the heart, but a single word in Chapter 1[:17], "In it the righteousness of God is revealed," that had stood in my way. For I hated that word "righteousness of God," which, according to the use and custom of all the teachers, I had been taught to understand philosophically regarding the formal or active righteousness, as they called it, with which God is

righteous and punishes the unrighteous sinner. Though I lived as a monk without reproach, I felt that I was a sinner before God with an extremely disturbed conscience. I could not believe that he was placated by my satisfaction. I did not love, yes, I hated the righteous God who punishes sinners, and secretly, if not blasphemously, certainly murmuring greatly, I was angry with God...Thus I raged with a fierce and troubled conscience. Nevertheless, I beat importunately upon Paul at that place, most ardently desiring to know what St. Paul wanted. At last, by the mercy of God, meditating day and night, I gave heed to the context of the words, namely, "In it [the gospel] the righteousness of God is revealed, as it is written, 'He who through faith is righteous shall live.'" There I began to understand that the righteousness of God is that by which the righteous lives by a gift of God, namely by faith. And this is the meaning: the righteousness of God is revealed by the gospel, namely, the passive righteousness with which merciful God justifies us by faith, as it is written, "He who through faith is righteous shall live." Here I felt that I was altogether born again and had entered paradise itself through open gates. There a totally other face of the entire Scripture showed itself to me. Thereupon I ran through the Scriptures from memory. I also found in other terms an analogy, as, the work of God, that is, what God does in us, the power of God, with which he makes us strong, the wisdom of God, with which he makes us wise, the strength of God, the salvation of God, the glory of God. And I extolled my sweetest word with a love as great as the hatred with which I had before hated the word "righteousness of God." Thus that place in Paul was for me truly the gate to paradise. Later I read Augustine's, where contrary to hope I found that he, too, interpreted God's righteousness in a similar way, as the righteousness with which God clothes us when he justifies us.[1]

This famous text from Luther's preface to the 1545 edition of his Latin works is interesting for our study not only because the Reformer regards an exegetical finding to be the core of the Reformation insight, but also because it makes us aware of the complexity of transmitting exegetical findings and bringing them to bear in systematic reflection. Augustine's words, which Luther regarded as confirming his insight, were quoted in Peter Lombard's widely distributed twelfth-century *Sentences*.[2] Peter repeated this point in his own words: "And as our righteousness is called righteousness of God, not because he himself is righteous by it, but because he makes us righteous by it, so also...."[3] Note, however, that, while Peter used this quotation from Augustine in order to explain the expression "*caritas Dei,*" he made no use of this Augustinian insight when he dealt with God's righteousness, where the basic problem is the relationship between God's mercy and God's righteousness from the perspective of the last judgment.

The comprehensive concept for medieval theologians was "righteousness," while "mercy" had to be explained within this framework. In his *Proslogion*, Anselm of Canterbury had offered a formula that was to be frequently quoted in times to come: "For when You punish the wicked, it is just, since it agrees with their merits; however, when You spare the wicked it is just, not because of their merits, but because it is befitting to Your goodness."[4] Anselm perceived God's justice according to his general concept of justice: "justice is the uprightness-of-will which is being kept for its own sake."[5] Thus, it is seen as an attribute rather than a gift of God as in Augustine. In his preface, Luther was referring to such systematic treatments of the "righteousness of God" as the phrase was understood in dogmatic treatises by the large majority of theologians. Here the Augustinian understanding was not the dominant one.

In the exegetical commentaries, on the other hand, one can find different motifs in understanding God's righteousness. Ambrosiaster, for example, treated it as an attribute of God; God's faithfulness and truthfulness in keeping promises. Pelagius took a different approach: God's righteousness is rewarding justice, with grace alongside of it. Augustine's understanding was distinct from both of these. Since Augustine emphasizes the power of God's grace and its effects, the righteousness of God is for him not an attribute but rather a gift of God. Later, these three motifs were mixed up frequently by a number of authors so that Augustine's understanding may be quoted but at the same time sidelined by the other two interpretations. Thus, the presence of the Augustinian concept does not, in itself, make an author's position Augustinian. Rather, one has to examine the understanding of God's righteousness as a whole composed of different strands. A crucial point is the interpretation of Rom 1:18, which speaks of the wrath of God just after God's righteousness is mentioned in 1:17. This prompts commentators to talk of "the other side of divine righteousness" so that the concept becomes ambiguous, even in biblical commentaries.

A striking example of this combination of views can be found in Aquinas's commentary on Romans. With reference to Rom 1:17 he mentions two meanings of the phrase "righteousness of God" without deciding for one over the other: (a) It can mean the righteousness by which God is righteous, with reference to Ps 11:7, or (b) the righteousness by which God justifies human beings. "For the righteousness of human beings is understood as the one by which they through their own powers claim to justify themselves, as Rom 10:3 says, 'being ignorant of the righteousness that comes from God, and seeking to establish their own, they have not submitted to God's righteousness.'"[6] But when it comes to the next verse, Rom 1:18 ["For the wrath of God is revealed from heaven against all ungodliness..."]), Aquinas declares without any explanation, "I say correctly that in it [the gospel] the righteousness of God is revealed, for in it the wrath of God is revealed, that is his punishment which is called 'wrath of God' according to a certain similarity with wrathful human beings who look for an external punishment."[7]

This history shows that Luther developed his understanding of "the righteousness of God" in a highly complex theological context. It is remarkable that when the Council of Trent came to define justification, they chose Augustine's formulation: "the one formal cause is the justness of God: not that by which he himself is just, but that by which he makes us just."[8]

2. By Faith Alone?

During the Reformation, Rom 3:28 ["For we hold that a person is justified by faith apart from works prescribed by the law"] was subject to controversy. In his German translation, Luther added "alone" after "by faith." He was sharply criticized for distorting the text and misleading people to think that they do not need to do good works. Luther defended his translation by (a) referring to a specific characteristic of the German language, and (b) by offering an exegetical argument. To point (a): "It is the nature of the German language to add the word *allein* in order that the word *nicht* or *kein* may be clearer and more complete. To be sure, I can also say, 'The farmer brings grain and *kein* money,' but the words '*kein* money' do not sound as full and clear as if I were to say, 'the farmer brings *allein* grain and *kein* money.' Here the word *allein* helps the word *kein* so much that it becomes a complete, clear German expression."[9] To point (b): Luther emphasized that he based his interpretation on the expression "without the works of the law":

> [T]he expression "faith alone" may perhaps be glossed over somehow, but the phrase "without the works of the law" is so blunt, offensive, and scandalous that no amount of interpretation can help it...I am amazed that anyone can take exception in a matter as evident as this. Just tell me: Is Christ's death and resurrection our work, that we do, or not? Of course it is not our work, nor the work of any law either. Now it is Christ's death and resurrection alone that saves us and makes us free from sin, as Paul says in Romans 4[:25]: "He died for our sins and rose for our justification." Tell me, further: What is the work by which we lay hold of Christ's death and resurrection? It cannot be any external work, but only the eternal faith that is in the heart. Faith alone, indeed, all alone, without any works, lays hold of this death and resurrection when it is preached through the gospel.[10]

Looking into the history of the interpretation of Rom 3:28, one can say that there is a vast consensus that it refers to justification by "faith alone" since it excludes the works of the law. The *sola fide* can be found explicitly in Origen's commentary, "He [Paul] says that justification by faith alone is sufficient, thus someone is justified by faith even though he may not have accomplished any single work."[11] Origen mentions the examples of the criminal on the cross (Luke 23:42–43) and the sinner of Luke 7:36–50. Nevertheless, with reference to Rom 4:1–8, Origen puts side by side the opinion that Abraham was justified by faith and a quotation of Jas 2:21–22, according to which Abraham was justified by faith that is brought to completion by works: "For it is sure that the true believer accomplishes the work of faith, of righteousness and of all-embracing goodness."[12]

Aquinas states that in Rom 3:28 works are excluded, and by referring to Titus 3:5 he explains that not only ritual works are meant. Furthermore, he explains that Paul speaks of the works prior to justification and not about later works that are explicitly required by Jas 2:26.[13]

After the Reformation, Roman Catholic theology in Germany could not deal with Rom 3:28 without taking Luther's translation into account. In the nineteenth century, Johann Adam Möhler did not reject Luther's translation of Rom 3:28 but rather the consequences that he saw Luther as having drawn from his theology of faith: "Luther added an 'alone' after *pistei*, 'faith.' This in itself does not need to be criticized since the genius of the German language allows for it—even requires it in order to express sharply the opposition. For this, Luther is not to be criticized, but rather for the fact that he not only misunderstood faith and the opposite of faith, but also made this misunderstanding the basis of his doctrine. For him, not only the works preceding justification are seen in opposition to faith but also the works that follow from it, so that his concept of justifying faith excluded the concept of love and *good* works."[14] To be sure, according to Luther's understanding faith is intimately connected with love and good works, as can be seen in his preface to Romans:

> Faith, however, is a divine work in us which changes us and makes us to be born anew from God, John 1[:12–13]. It kills the old Adam and makes us altogether different men, in heart and spirit and mind and powers; and brings with it the Holy Spirit. O it is a living, busy, active, mighty thing, this faith. It does not ask whether good works are to be done, but before the question is asked, it has already done them, and is constantly doing them. Whoever does not do such works, however, is an unbeliever....Faith is a living, daring confidence in God's grace, so sure and certain that the believer would stake his life on it a thousand times....it is impossible to separate works from faith, quite as impossible as to separate heat and light from fire.[15]

A more severe judgment came from a widely used twentieth-century scholastic textbook: "Luther got into an open contradiction to the Holy Scripture when he distorted Rom 3:28 by introducing the small word 'alone' and when he rejected the letter of James as an 'epistle of straw.'"[16]

3. Paul's Letter to the Romans and the Letter of James

The different interpretations of Rom 3:28 have already made it clear that the interpretation of this verse is connected to the understanding of the relationship between the Letter to the Romans and the Letter of James. Luther stated that there is a contradiction between Paul and James, and thus he marginalized James. These were his arguments: (a) James "is flatly against St Paul and all the rest of Scripture in ascribing justification to works [2:24]. It says that Abraham was justified by his works when he offered his son Isaac [2:21]; though in Romans 4[:2–22] St Paul teaches to the contrary that Abraham was justified apart from works, by his faith alone, before he had offered his son, and proves it by Moses in Genesis

15[:6]."¹⁷ (b) "In the second place its [the letter's] purpose is to teach Christians, but in all this long teaching it does not once mention the Passion, the resurrection, or the Spirit of Christ. He names Christ several times; however he teaches nothing about him, but only speaks of general faith in God. Now it is the office of a true apostle to preach of the Passion and resurrection and office of Christ, and to lay the foundation for faith in him, as Christ himself says in John 15[:27], 'You shall bear witness to me.' All the genuine sacred books agree in this, that all of them preach and inculcate [*treiben*] Christ. And that is the true test by which to judge all books, when we see whether or not they inculcate Christ."[18]

The problem of the relation between Paul's Letter to the Romans and the Letter of James played a certain role at the second Regensburg Colloquy, where Martin Bucer agreed that faith, love, and hope must belong together, as otherwise faith would be dead faith according to Jas 2:17. But since love and hope follow faith one cannot talk about merit here.[19] Bucer's Catholic opponents used James 2 as an argument for the doctrine that justification grows by means of good works.[20]

At the Council of Trent, there were discussions about the problem of works. The relation between Rom 3:24–28 ("apart from works of the law") and Rom 4:6 and Eph 2:9 ("apart from works") was much debated. In order not to have to clarify this problem, the words "apart from works (*sine operibus*)" were deleted from the decree (ch. 8), since an unqualified "apart from works" would contradict Jas 2:24.[21] The text of the Council clearly relates the works to be accomplished according to Jas 2:24–26 to the growth of the justification received,[22] while it states that "nothing that precedes justification, neither faith nor works, would merit the grace of justification."[23]

At the transition from the chapter on justification to the chapter on good works, the Second Helvetic Confession in 1566 explains the relationship between the Pauline doctrine of justification and James's sayings.

> Wherefore, in this matter we are not speaking of a fictitious, empty, lazy and dead faith, but of a living, quickening faith. It is and is called a living faith because it apprehends Christ who is life and makes alive, and shows that it is alive by living works. And so, James does not contradict anything in this doctrine of ours. For he speaks of an empty, dead faith of which some boasted but who did not have Christ living in them by faith (James 2:14ff.). James said that works justify, yet without contradicting the apostle (otherwise he would have to be rejected) but showing that Abraham proved his living and justifying faith by works. This all the pious do, but they trust in Christ alone and not in their own works" (ch. 15).[24]

Thus, we see three versions of the relationship between Romans and James: (1) opposition (Luther); (2) harmony because of the view that living faith does good works without the pursuit of merit (Bucer, Second Helvetic Confession); (3) harmony because of the insistence that the works of the justified contribute to the growth of justification (Möhler, Trent).

4. Romans 7

Concerning the interpretation of Romans 7, especially verses 14–25, there is a clear difference between the predominant strand of biblical interpretation over the last centuries and the interpretation of recent historical-critical exegesis. One of the main questions has always been, Who is the "I" that speaks in Romans 7? Many contemporary exegetes argue that, from the perspective of the apostle Paul, who has now become a Christian, the "I" refers to all human beings before grace. In contrast, for many early Christian theologians, Romans 7 refers to all human beings, including Christians after baptism and justification.[25] According to Origen, for example, in Romans 7 Paul speaks as a teacher who adopts the role of a pupil or a weak person in order to communicate with them in a pedagogically fruitful way. He understands the experiences mentioned in Romans 7 as the experiences of those "who have begun to convert."[26]

Augustine's development in this respect is revealing. For the early Augustine, Romans 7 speaks about the human being before grace. But later, in an anti-Pelagian move, he rejects this understanding as heretical.[27] A number of factors brought about this change of heart, including not only exegetical considerations but also broad systematic reflections and a range of personal and pastoral experiences in the imperial church of his day, which convinced him that grace had a lifelong struggle to prove its power in struggling with sin. Thus, an interpretation that exegetically might now seem to be shown false was existentially significant for people at the time.

After Augustine, this understanding remained for centuries the unquestioned standard interpretation. In his commentary on Romans, Aquinas applies both ways of understanding to Romans 7, while indicating the interpretation that refers the text to the Christian to be the better one.[28] In Catholic theology, this understanding continued to be held also after the Reformation and until the twentieth century.[29]

The problem with the exegesis of Romans 7 becomes especially acute when Luther's interpretation of this chapter is at stake. This chapter plays an important role in Luther's theology and in Lutheran theology overall, providing major exegetical evidence for the understanding that Christians are both righteous and sinners at the same time (*simul justus et peccator*). Thus, Luther's reflections are described here in some detail; they also provide a small case study of the relation between exegesis before the rise of historical-critical methods and exegesis as most contemporary exegetes would do it.

In arguing that the "I" in Romans 7 is the "I" of the apostle Paul, who speaks about himself, Luther quotes Augustine extensively and offers a series of arguments for his position. One argument claims that knowing oneself as "being of the flesh" is a sign of a spiritual person. Other arguments converge in Romans 7, identifying features of a spiritual person so that one must assume that Paul speaks about himself as a Christian. Luther thought of this alternative: Paul speaking about himself as a pre-Christian and in the person of any human being before justification, or speaking about himself as a Christian. He did not think of the possibility that Paul had anyone but Christians in mind while reflecting from the perspective of a Christian.

Since most theologians before Luther shared his understanding of the "I" in Romans 7, this cannot be the decisive point of his interpretation. His distinctive reading appears rather in the description and analysis of the conflict in which the Christian "I" is captured. Luther comments on Rom 7:15b–16b, "I do not do what I want, but I do the very thing I hate...I agree that the law is good": "From this we must not think that the apostle wants to be understood as saying that he does the evil which he hates, and does not do the good which he wants to, in a moral or metaphysical sense, as if he did nothing good but only evil, for in common parlance this might seem to be the meaning of his words. But he is trying to say that he does not do the good as often and as much and with as much ease as he would like. For he wants to act in a completely pure, free, and joyful manner, without being troubled by his rebellious flesh, and this he cannot accomplish."[30] In this understanding, Luther sees himself in agreement with Augustine. According to Augustine, Paul denies that the Christian as spirit could achieve a state in which concupiscence is not existent or active. While this is not possible, the Christian can prevent concupiscence from manifesting itself in a specific external act or work (*opus*). Since the Christian as spirit does not consent to concupiscence, he does not allow the flesh perfectly to perform its work but cannot eliminate its activity. On the other hand, the spirit cannot perfectly perform its will because concupiscence opposes it.

In the twentieth century, exegetes argued that this is not what Paul has in mind in Romans 7. After Paul, many factors, including monasticism, Augustinian influence, penitential exercises, and mysticism contributed to a new and deeper understanding of personhood that Luther took up and developed further so that his view is different from Paul's.

How can these processes be theologically evaluated? It does not suffice simply to state the historical fact. Can Luther's view be defended? Luther offers biblical arguments that compel him to go beyond Paul's thinking toward a deeper understanding of the reality of the Christian. We can analyze this development briefly in studying Luther's thesis, "That the righteous man also sins while doing good."[31] This thesis was as shocking for his contemporaries as it is for us today. But Luther offered proofs for it:

> This I shall prove by means of reason: Whoever does less than he ought sins. But every righteous person in doing good does less than he ought. Well, then, I shall prove the minor premise in the following way: Whoever does not do good out of complete and perfect love of God does less than he ought. But every righteous man is that kind of a person. I shall prove the major premise through

the commandment: "You shall love the Lord your God with all your soul, and all your might" etc. [Deut 6:5], of which the Lord says in Matt 5[:18], "Not an iota, not a dot, will pass from the law until all is accomplished." Therefore we must love God with all our might or we sin. But the minor premise, that we do not love him with all our might, has been proven above, for the unwillingness in the flesh and in the members hinders this perfection so that not all members or powers love God. This unwillingness resists the inner will which loves God.[32]

The crucial point is the understanding of the commandment of love of God. In the Middle Ages, it was generally understood that all works have eventually to be done out of love of God. But what does this mean when this love should be understood in line with the commandment, "You shall love the Lord your God with all your heart, and with all your soul, and with all your mind, and with all your strength" (Mark 12:30)? This problem is explicitly discussed by scholastic theologians such as Gabriel Biel, whose books Luther carefully studied.

Biel refers to Augustine's understanding of this commandment and summarizes his understanding as follows: "'You shall love God with all your heart etc.' is equivalent to You shall love God with all that is in you, and nothing in your thinking, longing, sense or work should be in you that is not subordinated to God, rather should everything be ordered towards him to whom it belongs."[33] Understood in this way, the commandment requires the dedication of the whole person to God. Therefore, it is highly astonishing that Biel states that the commandment can be summarized as saying, You shall love (*diligere*) God above all, while "*diligere*" in Biel's understanding is an act of the will, which is clearly different from the whole person. Contrary to Biel, Luther insists on the biblical commandment and claims that the whole person ***in all dimensions*** is challenged to be devoted to God. This is the will of God; this is the main content of the law. Since we are unable to fulfill the law understood in this spiritual way, we are and will remain sinners, even as Christians. It was this central biblical commandment that forced Luther to go beyond what we see in Paul, while Luther was convinced that he was faithfully interpreting the apostle. It should be added that, according to Luther, (a) the believer is made righteous by participating through faith in the fulfillment of the law by Jesus Christ and that therefore in relation to the gospel there is no condemnation against the believer; (b) faith and the Holy Spirit create new motions in a person with the effect that sin does not exercise dominion in the mortal bodies of the believers; thus (c) the law can be fulfilled by an act of will and a corresponding external act, but not with the dedication of the whole person, and thus not in the spiritual sense.

This very short review of Luther's arguments indicates that there were reasons for the Reformer to develop Paul's theology as he did. If we consider Luther's complex argumentation, we can reconstruct his theology even when we begin with a contemporary understanding of Paul. Lutherans will have to admit that there is a clear difference between some aspects of a historical-critical interpretation of Paul and Luther's understanding (Luther lived two hundred years before the emergence of a historical-critical awareness of the events and texts of the past). Living in an era different from Paul's and facing a different set of problems within the church, Luther was challenged to develop the doctrine further under the guidance of the command to love God. Therefore, this case provides an example that biblical texts have a surplus of meaning that goes beyond what they say in their original contexts.

5. Concluding Hermeneutical Remarks

All churches have the Bible in common. That should serve as a source of unity. Nevertheless, the different interpretations of the biblical texts have led to divisions within Christianity or at least have contributed to them. This chapter has presented some examples of these differences. Historical-critical research has created serious hope of overcoming these differences, since the method intends programmatically to interpret biblical texts in their respective contexts, which are explicitly or implicitly different from the traditions in which these texts have been understood so far. This going back behind traditions of interpretations to the original meaning of the biblical texts promises to contribute to Christian unity.

The ecumenical movement has in fact greatly benefited from historical-critical research. By merely reading an exegetical commentary, it is nowadays almost impossible to identify the church affiliation of its author. Historical-critical research has made theologians and churches aware that their respective traditions do not simply and fully represent the meaning of the biblical texts. This allows and calls for ecumenical conversations.

Moreover, this research has demonstrated the multiplicity of approaches that one can find in the Bible. This awareness opens the space for mutual enrichment between confessions, since they can realize that the distinctive ways in which they have understood the Bible may emphasize different aspects of the Bible but that they do not need to exclude or condemn one another. The canon of Scripture itself presents a model of unity in reconciled diversity and thus can serve and encourage looking for a similar unity among the church traditions, too.

Nevertheless, there are also problems in bringing exegetical findings to bear on systematic or constructive reflections. Catholic, Lutheran, Methodist, and Reformed Christians live from traditions that were developed with exegetical methods different from our contemporary ones. Thus, there are new challenges in demonstrating with these new methods how these traditions are rooted in the biblical message. Two aspects of these challenges may be mentioned.

Earlier theologians shared the presupposition of the basic unity of the Bible; thus, for example, the Book of Psalms could be used to interpret Paul's Letter to the Romans and vice versa. Historical-critical research intends to explore the specific profile of individual writings within the Bible and therefore does not primarily focus on the Bible's unity.

Even more serious is the consciousness of the difference between the time of the historian or interpreter and the time of the events investigated or the texts interpreted. Historical-critical research seeks to interpret the texts in their contexts, which lie far in the past. Thus, the present significance of these past texts becomes an urgent question. Earlier theologians did not have the consciousness that there was a huge divide between their world and the world of the Bible. They felt that they lived basically in the same world as the people of the Bible's time. This vision did not exclude the critical awareness that there had been developments between biblical times and their own. Luther, for example, was convinced that by overcoming medieval distortions he had reestablished a direct relation to the biblical books and regained the right understanding of the gospel. It spoke directly and immediately to the people of his time. He did not need to make huge efforts to bridge the gap between the time of the New Testament and the sixteenth century. In fact, he managed to merge the horizon of the Bible and that of his own time. He interpreted the Bible in the context of certain exegetical and doctrinal traditions that played a role in the sixteenth century, which he had received or rejected. He developed fresh insights into biblical texts that he had gained in a critical, controversial, or constructive encounter with the realities of church, state, society, culture, and their proponents in his time. Like Luther, other theological writers also related biblical texts to thoughts, experiences, and realities of their time that were at least partly different from those of the contexts in which the biblical texts originally had been written. However, from a contemporary standpoint, this merging resulted for some biblical texts in identifying a meaning different from their original meaning, at least as understood by present-day exegesis.

Does this mean that now we have to abandon a great part of the traditional interpretations because they differ from the original meaning? Instead, it is possible for contemporary readers to consider Luther's and other earlier theologians' exegesis as revealing "a surplus of meaning" of the biblical text. A feature of eminent texts generally is that their meaning is not limited to the meaning they have in their original setting. Readers have found meanings in the stories of Homer's *Odyssey,* for example, that the author himself would not have thought of. Moreover, the surplus of meaning in biblical texts also has a theological dimension. Since Scripture is the normative witness to the Word of God, it is not simply identified with this Word. The history of the church can, in some respects, be understood as the history of the interpretation of the Bible. In this history, Scripture unfolds its meaning and relevance for new and diverse contexts as interpreters continue to struggle with it. The multiplicity of confessional traditions of biblical interpretation can help to bring forth the surplus of meaning of biblical texts. In our time, different methods of biblical exegesis have been developed that attempt from a variety of perspectives to tease out different aspects of the meaning of these texts.

It does not, however, follow from this approach that every interpretation and tradition is consistent with the text. It is the task and achievement of biblical exegesis, not least of the historical-critical method, to identify reference points that can be used for testing the fidelity to the biblical witness of interpretations and traditions in the church. Therefore, it is ecumenically very important to reach a common understanding of the biblical message of the righteousness of God and the justification of human beings. The following chapters will attempt to outline such a common understanding.

IV

The Old Testament

1. Introduction

To understand the biblical doctrine of justification, we need to investigate the Old Testament witnesses to concepts, images, and narratives touching on righteousness, justice, and similar terms. In doing so, we will discover texts widely diverse in terms of language, date, and context. Some of these aspects of justification are well known because of their explicit reception within the New Testament; others may seem less familiar, but can inform a rich understanding of what goes on between God and humanity according to the witness of the whole Bible. This broader exploration will help us to understand better what the New Testament writers meant when they spoke about justification and God's righteousness.

Of course, we will also examine the texts that Paul and other New Testament writers used, noticing that the New Testament authors wrote in Greek and sometimes may have worked from a Greek translation (the Septuagint). All this is done acknowledging that we as Christian theologians today work from a Christian point of view yet are fully aware also that we share these Scriptures with Judaism and honor their place there.

Since there was no single, narrow perspective on justification in the Old Testament or in its subsequent reception by later generations, we have to try to take a very broad perspective and look as much as possible into all traditions represented in the writings of the Old Testament. What can we learn about God and about righteousness and justification from their different witnesses? In light of this perspective, we will not try to analyze and dissect all traditional and literary layers of the history of the Old Testament text. We will choose a thematic approach while recognizing the different situations to which different traditions speak.

We will consider first the righteousness of God, a notion central to the Old Testament but also basic to Paul's concept of justification, as is shown in Rom 1:17. We will then look at what the Old Testament writings say about the righteousness of the people of God, because it is often maintained that here we find a different understanding compared with Paul's and also the Reformation's doctrine of justification. Finally, we will ask what the Old Testament teaches about justification itself.

2. God's Righteousness

When we consider the Old Testament background to Christian notions of justification, we gravitate quite naturally to pivotal texts in Genesis and the Psalms, and to the most promising single term, Hebrew *ṣĕdāqāh* (often translated as "righteousness") in the hope of explicating not only the back matter but also the theological richness of the Greek word *dikaiosynē* (also translated as "righteousness") and extrapolated teachings about God's saving dispensation. The primary threads in our fabric take on hue and texture in Genesis, and then those threads lengthen and interweave through the balance of the Hebrew Scriptures in intriguing ways.

a. A cluster of terms and the real problem

We certainly need not limit ourselves to the single term *ṣĕdāqāh*, as the realities our narrators are trying to express emerge from a dumbfounded awe in search of language, inviting us to join them in a "raid on the inarticulate." While *ṣĕdāqāh* may be the Hebrew term most straightforwardly linked to the Greek word *dikaiosynē*, a *cluster* of terms cling to the theological and quite human realities being portrayed. The usage of any one term is interesting lexicographically and useful theologically; but when we broaden our investigation, we delight in a colorful tapestry that portrays something essential in the heart of God, and simultaneously at the epicenter of human existence. We will investigate such concepts associated with *ṣĕdāqāh* (righteousness) as *'ĕmûnāh (*faithfulness*), ḥesed (*steadfast love*), yāšār (right), mišpāṭ (justice), yēšā' (deliverance), 'ĕmet (faithfulness)* and their cognates, a bit embarrassed in advance that we are likely to miss a few others that would matter to the ancient writers.

The clustering of these terms is not our devising, but Scripture's own. Habitually these terms are arrayed together in varied contexts, from Psalms, prophets, and narrative. Let us consider Deut 32:4. This much-discussed "Song of Moses" eloquently offers a hymnic, creedal paean that ascribes greatness to "our God."

> The Rock, his work is perfect;
> for all his ways are justice (*mišpāṭ*).
> A God of faithfulness (*'ĕmûnāh*) and without iniquity,
> just (*ṣaddîq*) and right (*yāšār*) is he. (authors' translation)

The triumphal exuberance of such praise is tainted, vitiated, and engulfed in sorrow due to the pathetic human response that clangs noisily against the more fitting response of the praise itself:

> They have dealt corruptly with him,
> they are no longer his children because of their blemish;
> they are a perverse and crooked generation. (Deut 32:5, authors' translation)

It seems that the perennial bad news is that the *ṣĕdāqāh, 'ĕmûnāh, ḥesed, yāšār,* and *mišpāṭ* of God, which God does not merely possess but also pours out in abundance, are met with human stupidity, refusal, and perversion.

This contrast is the problem. In a way, the entire Old Testament is about the rectification of precisely this dilemma in which we—and God!—find ourselves. Something is true about God; there is a dream, a hope, a luxuriant goodness, which we glimpse down here from time to time. But too often, perpetually and tragically, what is in God is not mimicked, not echoed, not embodied, as God would wish and as the people so desperately need, in the life of the community and world.

The basis of and the hope for righteousness are in the nature of God. Righteousness begins in creation itself, and the splendor of creation is the best metaphor of the heart of God. Creation itself proclaims God's *ṣedeq* (Ps 97:6). Psalm 36:5–6 puts a cluster of terms on display that characterize the creative power and goodness of God:

> Your steadfast love (*ḥesed*), O LORD, extends to the heavens,
> your faithfulness (*'ĕmûnāh*) to the clouds.
> Your righteousness (*ṣĕdāqāh*) is like the mighty mountains,
> your judgments (*mišpāṭ*) are like the great deep;
> you save (*yš'*) humans and animals alike, O LORD.

God's righteousness has a cosmic dimension. God's creation and sustaining of the world are also expressions of God's righteousness. That which gives the community of persons order and security also gives the natural world constancy and prosperity. Psalm 33:4–6 substantiates its call to praise God in this way:

> For the word of the LORD is upright,
> and all his work is done in faithfulness.
> He loves righteousness and justice;
> the earth is full of the steadfast love of the LORD.
> By the word of the LORD the heavens were made,
> ...and all their host by the breath of his mouth.

Thus, righteousness also means the salvific "world order" that unites cosmic, political, religious, social, and ethical aspects. This was not only a concept of ancient Israel. It embraces elements of ancient Middle Eastern presuppositions, particularly characteristics of Ma'at, the Egyptian goddess of wisdom and order.

But although righteousness, just like peace or faithfulness or grace, sometimes seems to be an almost separate entity, it is an integral part of what is seen as the nature of the one God of Israel. The best example of this is Ps 85:9–13:

> Surely his salvation is at hand for those who fear him,
> That his glory may dwell in our land.
> Steadfast love and faithfulness will meet;
> Righteousness and peace will kiss each other.
> Faithfulness will spring up from the ground,
> and righteousness will look down from the sky.
> The LORD will give what is good, and our land will yield its increase.
> Righteousness will go before him, and will make a path for his steps.

Here not only the creation and preservation of the world are expressions of the righteous actions of God but also fruitfulness and prosperity (cf. also Pss 65:5–13; 72:16; Hos 2:18–22).

This concept of the "cosmic" aspect of the righteousness of God is indissolubly connected with God's concern for social justice. It is the king as God's representative who is expected to mediate God's righteousness to his people. Psalm 72:1–4 therefore prays:

> Give the king your justice, O God,
> and your righteousness to a king's son.
> May he judge your people with righteousness,
> and your poor with justice.
> May the mountains yield prosperity for the people,
> and the hills, in righteousness.
> May he defend the cause of the poor of the people,
> give deliverance to the needy, and crush the oppressor.

All these wonders are not mystical secrets, but are loudly proclaimed.

> The LORD has made his salvation (*yĕšûʿāh*) known;
> In the sight of the nations has revealed his justice (*ṣĕdāqāh*);
> He has remembered his kindness (*ḥesed*) and faithfulness (*ʾĕmûnāh*).
> (Ps 98:2–3, authors' translation)

Many other Psalms deploy combinations of these terms (Pss 143:1–12; 145:7–9; 146:5–7), and those who prayed delighted in extolling this saving, gracious disposition of God:

> I have told the glad news of deliverance (*ṣedeq*) in the great
> congregation;
> I have not hidden your saving help (*ṣĕdāqāh*) within my heart, ...

I have spoken of your faithfulness (*'ĕmûnāh*) and your salvation
(*tĕšû'āh*);
I have not concealed your steadfast love (*ḥesed*).... (Ps 40:9–10)

In fact, one sorrow of death will be the inability to proclaim God's steadfast love, faithfulness, and saving help (Ps 88:11–12).

b. Righteousness as relational

Righteousness might sound like some absolute standard of rightness, but the texts just cited underline what nearly every major study has identified: the primarily relational nature of righteousness. Almost no texts imply that God's righteousness is punitive or forensic. God's gracious, generous relationship to the people is the righteousness of God. And the relational nature of righteousness does not stop with God: it is to be mimicked, embodied in relationships among the people who benefit from God's righteousness. The vertical and horizontal intersection of divine and social righteousness is, in fact, the blessed life of the people of Israel.

Sin and guilt are usually associated with other terminology, such as *nāqām*, *kālāh*, or *pāqād*. Righteousness, on the other hand, is linked to *yeša'*, God's saving gift of deliverance (Isa 45:8; 51:5–7; 63:1; Pss 65:6; 71:2; Zech 9:9). *ṣĕdāqāh* is first something about God, something God not only is but achieves, commits to, and then (hopefully) those restored and saved by it reflexively mimic and embody this *ṣĕdāqāh*. Perhaps this is revealed in a lovely way by the unusual plural usage in 1 Sam 12:7 and Judg 5:11, where *ṣĕdāqôt* means something like "saving deeds," for which the people glorify God. Righteousness might be defined as Yahweh's readiness to intervene and be present in time, to rehabilitate, restore, and bring shalom. So the fascinating doxological proclamations in Judg 5:11 and 1 Sam 12:7 are thus interventions that made possible what was not otherwise possible. When considering the doctrine of justification, we may rightly be tantalized by these suggestive nuances of *ṣĕdāqāh* as something about God, as God's saving deeds—not the achievement that elicited the people's election but a beneficial reality becoming palpable in the life of the people, despite their manifest failures in echoing *ṣĕdāqāh*, and raising the urgency for a life deemed *ṣaddîq*.

The distinction between *ṣedeq* and *ṣĕdāqāh* also makes a difference. *Ṣedeq* carries the sense of the abstract right order of the universe, God's providence and governance, and God's salvational or vindicating actions on behalf of God's people. It is the firm order that is established and to be observed—kings, in particular, and judges, must act according to *ṣedeq* (Ps 45:8; Prov 31:9). Zion and its king can both be titled "God our righteousness" in Jeremiah's vision of a new Jerusalem (Jer 23:6; 33:16). This basic sense of an order, faithful to God's intention, is summed up by Ps 35:24, "Vindicate me, O LORD, my God, according to your righteousness (*ṣĕdāqāh*)." The feminine noun, *ṣĕdāqāh*, seems to refer to the specific actions of *ṣedeq* in action. It often specifies God's salvational intervention for the people or God's actions to maintain his right rule over the world (see Deut 6:25; Isa 54:17; Ps 103:6). God also bestows it on individuals, such as on Abraham in Gen 15:6 or on Phineas in Ps 106:31 because God made a promise to them in which they believed.

Righteousness is relational—not only on God's side but among people. God wishes God's own relational righteousness to be mirrored in the life of the people. Human beings also practice ṣĕdāqāh because they wish to retain the right relationship with God. At least twenty times the expression is used "to do righteousness (and justice)." Thus, the primary difference between ṣedeq and ṣĕdāqāh is that the former is primarily used of divine order and purpose, while the latter emphasizes the activity of doing what is ṣedeq.

We can see this relational dynamic in the Ten Commandments, which provide an important summary of God's instruction to Israel. The first commandments spell out some of what it means to love God with one's whole heart. The rest describe the responsibilities of God's people to one another. The entirety of the Torah, according to the narrative of the Pentateuch, was given after God had delivered the people from Egypt. The "Law" was not the means to divine deliverance. Rather, it was a result of God's saving action. Thus, the commandments provide a guide for how Israel could best live the quality of life God desired for them, and thrive in their relationship with God and with one another: that we can call "righteousness."

c. Related terms—faithfulness, steadfast love, rightness, and justice

In our texts, we notice that ṣĕdāqāh has quite a few friends, such as 'ĕmûnāh (faithfulness), ḥesed (steadfast love), yōšer (rightness), and mišpāṭ (justice), all of which are pertinent for a holistic understanding of justification. 'ĕmûnāh, "faithfulness," is something God has and the people lack (Deut 32:20). Yet when a person acts in faithfulness ('ĕmûnāh), there can be great reward (as in 1 Sam 26:23). Another significant term that bears discussion is mišpāṭ. In Exodus 21, often in Leviticus and other legal materials, and in narrative contexts (1 Sam 30:25), mišpāṭ is an ordinance, something God requires; the prelude to the Shema uses the plural mišpāṭîm, the teachings that God told Moses to articulate so that the people might possess the land and have life. The plural is also often used when the texts refer to collections of the "ordinances" of God (Exod 21:1; Deut 4:1; 5:1).

Israel's prophets also utilize this concept of justice as faithfulness to the statutes of God. A person is faithful to God in living and practicing just and fair relations (Hab 2:4). Israel's unfaithfulness, however, led to injustice and the need for a new covenant (Hos 2:20–25; Isa 9:6; 11:4–9; 16:5). But, at the same time, through the light of faithful prophets, God continues to call Israel to just and righteous living. These are not random, free-floating laws, but something more personal, the requirements of a personal relationship, since "all God's ways are *mišpāṭ*" (Deut 32:4).

Human stewards are charged with dispensing this *mišpāṭ*, which is properly God's. People came to Deborah, sitting under a palm tree, for *mišpāṭ* (Judg 4:5). So highly valued was this *mišpāṭ* that when people came to Absalom for it, he was able to "steal their hearts" (2 Sam 15:2–6). The failure to deliver *mišpāṭ* was especially despicable; Samuel's sons "did not walk in his ways, but turned aside after gain; they took bribes and perverted *mišpāṭ*" (1 Sam 8:3, authors' translation).

In a way, *mišpāṭ* involves restraint on this issue of "gain." A steady chorus of texts raises the bar for Israel: judgment cannot be unjust, or partial, or deferential to the rich (Lev 19:15; Deut 1:17; 16:19). Somewhat shockingly, there is a single *mišpāṭ* for Israel and for the sojourner (Lev 24:22; Num 15:16); small and great alike are heard. Bias toward the haves is upended; the have-nots may have nothing else, but they will have *mišpāṭ*. *Mišpāṭ* inspires and settles for no less than a radical leveling, and the uncomfortable de-privileging of those who are canny enough to get ahead. Such an arrangement is not a liberal quest for fairness or equality: rather, this style of *mišpāṭ* simply mirrors the heart and mind of God, and keeping *mišpāṭ* gives life to the people (Deut 4:1; 6:20).

This whole issue is also central to the accusations of the early prophets. They blame God's people that *mišpāṭ* and *ṣĕdāqāh* are no longer found in its midst, and therefore the poor, the orphans, and the widows suffer from exploitation and marginalization. In the Book of Isaiah, justice is seen as a gift from God (Isa 1:27; 45:8), which is made evident by a just way of life (Isa 1:17; 58:2–14). Amos makes the absence of justice the center of his prophetic accusation against Israel (Amos 5:7; 6:12). The other prophets joined him to denounce the injustice against fellow beings as a bloody form of unbelief and idolatry. The leaders of the nation promoted and participated in the oppression of the poor of the land. Although they did not reject and renounce the covenant outright, they were still disloyal to God. They acted like other nations, who followed gods that demanded human victims to satisfy their wrath.

Amos stresses God's moral rule over the entire world and the divine demand for justice and concern for the outcast and the oppressed. Amos connects the injustice he sees around him to a society bent on wealth and prosperity and forgetful of the true worship of God. Oppression of the poor is an unmistakable sign of ill will and offense to God. God is the defender of the poor, loyal to those in need of fair treatment. The prophets clearly warn that a good relationship with God is impossible when fellow beings are being treated unjustly (Hos 10:4, 11–15; 12:7–8; Amos 2:6; 5:11; Isa 5:23; Mic 6:11–12). This helps us to understand why God rejected all insincere worship and sacrifice, all hypocritical religion: it does not demonstrate fair dealings with one's fellow beings. Hosea could see the effects of apostasy on the morals of society, as injustice and dishonesty increased, and he therefore emphasized the need to live up to the commandments of Yahweh.

On the eve of the deportation of the people by the Babylonians, the prophets Jeremiah and Ezekiel saw justice from the perspective of loyalty to God (Jer 3:11; 5:3–5; 22:3; Ezek 16:51). Although the people were taken into captivity, God, who is faithful to God's covenant, preserves a remnant of the people who are faithful. The prophetic messages that call the people to return to God and renew their covenant with God show that conversion is necessary. This return to God is intended to establish God's justice. Conversion, therefore, becomes the way to return to a just relationship with God. Conversion makes justice personal and involves us in the establishment of justice (Jer 4:1; Zeph 2:3; Ezek 14:14; 18:5–9, 14–17, 20; Hab 2:4).

What we see in these texts regarding justice is that God has a powerful inclination toward lifting up the have-nots. While Israel is encouraged to do well by the have-nots, Israel also discovers that in reality they are the have-nots. They are in need of not merely a kind of mercy but a truer sort of justice, *mišpāṭ*, in which God fortunately de-privileges but also raises up. Thus, God's vision for a particular kind of community is articulated and embodied. Is justification not something about de-privileging and then raising up, a gift God simply insists the people have?

An obviously promising term in the "righteousness" discussion is *ḥesed*. Meaning something like "abiding covenant fidelity," *ḥesed* is not used very often in the Pentateuch, and only a bit more in the Deuteronomistic history. In Exod 34:6 (as in Num 14:18), we see *ḥesed* as a major element in Israel's confessional set pieces; *ḥesed* is the very character of God and is often linked to pardon and mercy. In 2 Sam 7:15, God even calls it "my steadfast love" (*ḥasdî*). *Ḥesed* is the instrument whereby God guides the people out of slavery (Exod 15:13). It is something God "shows" (*'āśāh*) or "keeps" (*nāṣar* or *šāmar*); *ḥesed* is a commitment within God, but one that emanates out toward God's people (Exod 20:6; 34:7; Deut 5:10; 7:9, 12; 1 Kgs 8:23).

On the other hand, it is *ḥesed*, the deep and affectionate love of the people as a response to the love God has shown to them, that God desires from his people rather than sacrifice and burnt offerings (Hos 6:6; cf. 4:1).

A relational term carrying deep personal, emotional freight, *ḥesed* characterizes an especially intimate friendship (2 Sam 16:17). Political nuances were inevitable, since so much of the Deuteronomist's story is about rivals and factions (2 Sam 3:8; 9:1, 7; 10:2; 1 Kgs 2:7). The most pivotal slant on *ḥesed* in such contexts would be when a warrior "deals kindly" with the vanquished; it is for *ḥesed* that Rahab pleads; and in Judg 1:24; 1 Sam 15:6; 20:8, 14; and 2 Sam 2:5, we see *ḥesed* in the merciful treatment of the vulnerable in embattled times; restraint in killing spills over into gestures of kindness and hospitality (2 Sam 2:5; 3:8; 9:1), especially in the instance of David's kindness to Mephibosheth. This sort of merciful, undeserved but sorely needed hospitality fits quite well with what the recipients of *ḥesed* would experience, and all would then be set right (*yāšār*), and ṣĕdāqāh would dawn. Could a narrative image of justification be the unexpected survival and blessed life of Mephibosheth?

Perhaps most interesting is *yāšār*, meaning "straight, smooth, right." If Yahweh is *yāšār*, then that "rightness" finds itself mirrored in human existence. The cows pulling the ark went "straight" to Bethshemesh, veering neither right nor left. The Gibeonites tell Joshua to do what seems "right" in your mind to us (Josh 9:25); Samuel instructs the people in what is good and "right" (1 Sam 12:23). Jehonadab and Jehu agree that their hearts are *yāšār* ("true" or "loyal") to one another (2 Kgs 10:15). This usage in human relationship takes on warm resonances: news that Michal loved David "pleased" Saul (1 Sam 18:20), just as being Saul's son-in-law "pleased" David (1 Sam 18:26).

If the Lord is *yāšār* and *yōšer* is a vital aspect of human existence, we may attend to what *yāšār* looks like between God and the people. Conditional nuances, as in Exod 15:26; Deut 6:18; 12:25; 13:18; 1 Kgs 11:33; 14:8 ("if you do what is *yāšār* in God's eyes, you will avoid disease, possess the land, or keep the kingdom") become the foil for mercy; while Ahaz and a gallery of rogue kings failed to do what was *yāšār* in God's eyes, the Israelites could always look back to their founding days, when it was "not because of *yōšer* of heart were you able to possess the land" (Deut 9:5, authors' translation). Indeed, when the occasional king rises to the level of *yōšer* (Hezekiah, Josiah), the spin on that reign is less heroic than one of relief, or the realization of something beyond human capacity; God's goodness dawned in those days. Some paradox is afoot here: while Deut 9:5 can say it is not due to *yōšer* that the land was possessed, Deut 6:18 quite clearly requires *yōšer* in order for the land to be had. Behind this paradox, we may discover a development within the genesis of Deuteronomy, which points more and more to a theology of God's unconditional grace and makes this book of the Old Testament a witness to an Old Testament version of the message of justification in its own right.

Delving more deeply into Deuteronomy, we see that *yōšer* is not some independent entity, some property one has or does (or fails to have or do). The purging of guilt is a benefit of doing what is *yāšār* "in God's eyes" (Deut 21:9), whereas when human beings do what is *yāšār* in their own eyes catastrophe strikes. Indeed, the darkest eras of Israel's history were not when people set their hearts on wickedness, but rather on what was *yāšār* in their own eyes (Judg 17:6); the very last sentence of the Book of Judges is precisely this gloomy assessment: "Every man did what was *yāšār* in his own eyes" (Judg 21:25, authors' translation). So *yōšer* has no independent substance, but has an author, a personal trustee—and the habitual routine is that the divine *yōšer* is twisted perversely by human beings who strut out quite proudly their own *yōšer*, which is a mere parody of God's. This wrinkle in the Deuteronomistic deployment of *yōšer* may be a fruitful line of inquiry for what Paul and then Christendom did with the doctrine of justification; a profusion of seeming human goodness may be nothing more than a parody of what God desires.

Proverbs 12:15 sounds a similar warning: "The way of a fool is right in his own eyes, but a wise man listens to advice" (authors' translation). And Qoheleth tells his audience not to be overly wise and make oneself overly righteous (Eccl 7:16). Absolute righteousness belongs to God. Real righteousness on the side of human beings has its source always in God!

In these reflections on *ṣedeq*, *'ĕmûnāh*, *ḥesed*, *yāšār*, and *mišpāṭ*, we might detect a bit of a melody emerging from the various notes sounded. The character of God, celebrated in Deut 32:4, should fuel the reality of human life, ours with God, ours with each other. But with relentless zeal, God's people do what is right in their eyes, which only leads to injustice and the crumpling of their own vitality, cut off as they make themselves from God's ways. Yet God never simply torches them or abandons them, but just as relentlessly clings to a disposition to bring the people back, and to press on for the day, or even brief glimpses of the day, when God's ways would be realized on earth. No human virtue elicits this from God; it is sheer goodness, a consistency in the psyche of God that brings hope.

3. The Righteousness of the People of God

a. Human ability and disability

Throughout the Old Testament, we sense a genuine expectation that human beings have abilities to do what God asks; expectations are high, and are not intended to demoralize. Worshipers about to enter the temple are told that those with clean hands and pure hearts will receive vindication (*ṣĕdāqāh*); so clean hands and pure hearts must be a possibility (Ps 24:5). Many Psalms cry out in innocence to God, pleading with God to justify those who are innocent, confident that God will do so; Ps 37:5–6 urges, "Commit your way to the Lord, trust in him, and he will act. He will make your vindication (*ṣedeq*) shine like the light, and the justice (*mišpāṭ*) of your cause like the noonday." Indeed, declarations of innocence, either autobiographical, or when one testifies on behalf of another, claim righteousness while invoking the divine imprimatur on that righteousness. Judah claims that Tamar is "more in the right (*ṣādĕqāh mimmenni*)" (Gen 38:26), and thus the stigma of what had seemed being in the wrong is lifted.

Another such cluster of terms, not lauding the heart of God but highlighting the virtues of one of God's people, is found in 1 Kgs 3:6.

> And Solomon said, "You have shown great and steadfast love (*ḥesed*) to your servant my father David, because he walked before you in faithfulness (*be'ĕmet*), in righteousness (*biṣdāqāh*), and in uprightness (*bĕyišrat*) of heart toward you; and you have kept for him this great and steadfast love (*ḥesed*)."

Admittedly, some pompous braggadocio is in play, but the Old Testament doggedly retains a modest optimism about the possibility of faithful human responsiveness to God.

But the general outlook is bleak indeed (Job 32:1–2), and quite often the Old Testament takes a dim view of human nature and exposes the crass inability of human beings to enact the righteousness God is and gives. Qoheleth's gloomy assessment, "Surely there is not a righteous man on earth" (Eccl 7:20 RSV), is echoed in the cadences of negative verdicts on kings and people throughout the Deuteronomistic history, and the Psalms lament that we are worms and that "I was born guilty, a sinner when my mother conceived me" (Ps 51:5).

Thus, we have a two-sided picture in the Old Testament. On the one hand, many Psalms cry out in innocence to God, pleading with God to justify those who are innocent, confident that God will do so (Ps 37:5). People who pray to God in this way would not claim that their righteousness is in full correspondence with the will of God. But in view of those who accuse them unjustly they plead their innocence regarding these accusations.

On the other hand, there are Psalms that give voice to those who have to confess: "If you, O Lord, should mark iniquities, Lord, who could stand?" (Ps 130:3; cf. 51:3–14). But the remarkable thing is that both—those who call themselves righteous and those who see themselves as sinners—appeal to God's righteousness (compare Pss 31:1; 35:23–24 with 40:10–11; 143:1–2), and have nothing else to depend upon.

b. Mediators of righteousness

The people are to embody this cluster of realities, righteousness, faithfulness, steadfast love, uprightness, and justice. Nonetheless, there are some key personnel who bear a particular responsibility as leaders, midwives of righteousness, stewards of the practical realities that issue from this comprehensive life of righteousness. God appointed priests, prophets, judges, and even kings and sages who articulate the blunt truths and subtle nuances of righteousness, pioneer the implementation of a righteous, just society, and mercifully offer the necessary mechanisms for restoration, the justification of the unrighteous.

Not surprisingly, since we see that the people are capable of fulfilling what God desires and yet are simultaneously and pathetically incapable of a consistent righteousness, we understand the need for righteous leaders, and the sorrowful chagrin caused by their foibles, which seem to exceed even that of the people at large.

Consider the judges, whose very title, *šōpĕṭîm*, underlines their grave responsibility for *mišpāṭ*. As we saw earlier, Deborah sat under a palm tree, where the people came to her for *mišpāṭ* (Judg 4:5). Even the *šōpĕṭîm*, who were military heroes, were stirred into action partly due to a failure of *mišpāṭ*. Such failure to provide *mišpāṭ* was catastrophic, as in the case of Samuel's sons (1 Sam 8:3).

The priests were, in a way, the most essential purveyors of righteousness, through word and administration of sacrifice, making provision for justification. They also served as judges. The instructional and judicial functions of the priesthood brought priests into contact with the people through their role as those who taught the people the Torah (instruction), the correct procedures in religious and legal matters. But their record of fidelity is ambivalent at best, Eli's sons appearing early in Israel's saga as tawdry abusers of their office: "worthless men," they sinned egregiously by pilfering the sacrificial meat (1 Sam 2:17).

Kings, naturally, were granted a wide berth in the administration of divine realities like righteousness and justice. The eloquent liturgy spoken at their anointing (Psalm 72), forcefully enjoining *mišpāṭ* and *ṣĕdāqāh* upon the newly crowned, was swiftly forgotten by a rapid succession of failed kings. One could argue that the primary function of the prophets was not, first of all, to summon the people back to covenant loyalty, but to expose the shenanigans of royalty.

The prophetic office spoke truth to power, denouncing the obstruction and perversion of righteousness: "Woe to him who builds his house by unrighteousness (*bĕlō'-ṣedeq*), and his upper rooms by injustice (*lō'-mišpāṭ*)....Did not your father…do justice (*mišpāṭ*) and righteousness (*ṣĕdāqāh*)?…He judged the cause of the poor and needy" (Jer 22:13–16). Yet the prophets themselves were not an undiluted bunch. The specter of false prophecy that gave blanket endorsement to unrighteous kings spoiled trust and God's dream for the people: "I did not send the prophets, yet they ran; I did not speak to them, yet they prophesied" (Jer 23:21).

Little wonder that the demands of these offices came to be transmuted into a future hope. Today's king might fail, but one day God will raise up one who knows and does God's will. "Behold, the days are coming when I will raise up for David a righteous (*ṣaddîq*) branch, and he shall reign and deal wisely and shall execute justice (*mišpāṭ*) and righteousness (*ṣĕdāqāh*) in the land" (Jer 23:5–6, authors' translation); "With righteousness (*bĕṣedeq*) he shall judge (*šāpaṭ*) the poor, and decide with equity for the meek of the earth; righteousness (*ṣedeq*) shall be the girdle of his waist, and faithfulness (*'ĕmûnāh*) the girdle of his loins" (Isa 11:4–5, authors' translation).

A special class of mediator would be the sage. Quite a few proverbs counsel the young and those who would be wise to do righteousness (*ṣĕdāqāh*). *Ṣĕdāqāh* occurs largely in proverbs in parallel with a similar or contrasting value. The general characteristic of these constructions emphasizes general attitudes or ways of life rather than a concrete act of evil or judgment. Thus, in the examples that follow, several accent the contrast between the ongoing pursuit of wealth and true righteousness, or see righteousness as a path or way of living. It is a quality of good kingship (see Psalm 72) in all that he does, and a guard for a lifelong quest of complete innocence and wholeness with God. This righteousness is much more an enduring quality of relationship with God. It is moral uprightness and a commitment to obey God's commands, but it is never associated with a specific concrete command of the Torah.

Consider this sampling of sage counsel regarding *ṣĕdāqāh*: "Evil riches do not profit, but *ṣĕdāqāh* delivers from death" (Prov 10:2, authors' translation).

"Wealth does not profit on the day of trouble, but *ṣĕdāqāh* delivers from death" (Prov 11:4, authors' translation). "Whoever sows *ṣĕdāqāh* has a true reward" (Prov 11:18, authors' translation). "*Ṣĕdāqāh* exalts a nation, but sin is a reproach to any people" (Prov 14:34). "Better a little in *ṣĕdāqāh* than great income without *mišpāṭ*" (Prov 16:8, authors' translation). "To do *ṣĕdāqāh* and *mišpāṭ* is better than sacrifice" (Prov 21:3, authors' translation). It is as if *ṣĕdāqāh* is not a stand-alone concept, but always defines itself in contrast to what happens all too often in the fallen, wayward world of Israel.

The residue of the teachings of the sages is the wisdom literature, in which we find even deeper probing into the realities of righteousness. The Book of Job provides a fascinating perspective on righteousness, as it explores the very meaning of being righteous. Job and his friends argue the case in terms of both general attitudes (self-righteousness) and specific sins of which Job is either ignorant or which he refuses to admit. Thus, much more than in Proverbs, there are strong overtones of the legal implications. To be *ṣaddîq* is to be in the right before God, having confessed wrongdoing and accepted divine forgiveness. Much of the argument among the friends centers on whether Job is deserving of divine punishment for not being righteous. This argument of the Book of Job could lead to an association of fidelity to the Torah and divine vindication or punishment.

However, we should note that in all three places where God directly challenges Job's claims to being righteous, he does so on the grounds that Job has gone beyond his human ability or right to know God's purposes, and so his major lack of righteousness is his hubris in thinking he can challenge God on the grounds of what is *ṣedeq* in God's plan. True knowledge of God is found not in human intelligence, which interprets divine order according to our standards, but in submission to and recognition of God's lordship over the universe, even when it seems to be unfair or beyond our comprehension. A catalogue of queries and laments in Job gives us the feel of righteousness, and its purported existence, in human life: "How can a person be considered just (*yiṣdaq*) before God?" (Job 9:2, authors' translation). "Even if I were in the right (*ṣādaqtî*), I could not respond, I would seek my *mišpāṭ*" (Job 9:15, authors' translation). "The *ṣaddîq*, the wholehearted, is a joke" (Job 12:4, authors' translation). "The *ṣaddîq* holds fast to his way" (Job 17:9, authors' translation). "I am clothed with *ṣedeq*, my robe and turban are my *mišpāṭ*" (Job 29:14, authors' translation). Job insists on his own righteousness, refusing to untether his exasperation from his sense of being righteous (Job 27:5); he even dares to appeal to God against God (Job 16:19–21; 19:25–26). And, indeed, in the end, God does ultimately pronounce him righteous. The way Job speaks of *ṣedeq* and *mišpāṭ* in such picturesque, personal terms tells us volumes about the intense engagement the Israelites felt in their relationship with God.

c. Righteousness "reckoned" by God

It is noteworthy that this human righteousness is not moral rectitude or flawless adherence to the commandments. Tamar is cornered into an act of seduction, but then Judah praises her: "You are more righteous than I (*ṣādĕqāh mimmenni*)" (Gen 38:26, authors' translation). Her "righteousness" is her rightful place in the community, the essential need of the justice denied her; so whatever shame that might attach itself to her act is shed.

Clearly, any hint of pious sanctimony is excluded. To be righteous in one's own eyes is despicable to the Lord. Proverbs echoes this melody: "The way of a fool is right in his own eyes, but a wise man listens to advice" (Prov 12:15, authors' translation). Only God can make a person or the people righteous; righteousness, even when practiced faithfully, is a gift of God. And the basis of human goodness resides outside the person. Late in Israel's journey with God we read: "We do not present our supplication on the ground of our righteousness (*ṣĕdāqôt*), but on the ground of your great mercies" (Dan 9:18).

The foundational event of this mercy is the exodus, and the precursor to that salvational deliverance is the story of Abraham. Genesis 15:6 is, certainly for Paul, the most spectacular instance of the way "righteousness" happens. Translating the Hebrew poses some initial challenges:

> And he believed in the LORD; and he counted it to him for righteousness (KJV).
> Abram put his faith in the LORD, who credited it to him as an act of righteousness (NAB).
> Abram put his faith in Yahweh and this was reckoned to him as uprightness (NJB).
> And Abram believed the LORD, and the LORD declared him righteous because of his faith (NLT).
> And he believed the LORD; and the LORD reckoned it to him as righteousness (NRSV).
> And because he put his trust in the LORD, He reckoned it to his merit (TNK).

In this passage, the translation of *ṣĕdāqāh* has been rendered in several different ways in English biblical translations. This suggests that linguists are drawing on an extended *Wortfeld* (semantic field) for the Hebrew term. It also means that there may be legitimate disagreements among such experts about the proper sense of the word. Such uncertainty should help discover perhaps a broader meaning than either a legal or a moral usage, the two most common interpretations.

In this narrative, Abraham's faith becomes exemplary for the future generations. To keep hold of God's promises even in difficult times is "reckoned" by God as righteousness. This view receives support from the context of chapter 15 as a whole, which contains two encounters between God and Abraham and a concluding scene (Gen 15:1–6, 7–17, 18–21). In verses 1–6, Abraham questions the promise God had given in 12:1–3 that he would become a great nation (*gôy gādôl*), since he had no heir. In verses 7–17, God addresses the promise of land that he will bestow on Abraham's descendants. Both are then answered when God deepens the promise of 12:1–3 into a formal covenant, expressly stating in Gen 15:18 that God will "cut a covenant" (*kārat bĕrît*) (authors' translation) that combines the promise of descendants and land into one statement. The three scenes together situate Abraham in a typical ancient Near Eastern covenant setting in which the solemn ratification of the treaty is symbolized by the splitting and passage between parts of an animal.

The structure of Genesis 12–25 is presented as a foreshadowing of the covenant relationship to be established definitively at Sinai. Many narrative similarities exist between the Abraham story and Exodus 1–24 (Numbers 11–20). An individual (or a people) is called from a land, not subject to obedience to God, to journey to a new land, where God awaits them to establish a new relationship; the journey is motivated by a promise of prosperity and nationhood (Gen 12:1–3; Exod 3:1–15); doubt sets in (Gen 15:1–15; Exodus 16–18); God reaffirms the promise by also offering a covenant relationship (Gen 15:1–21; Exodus 19–24); and the relationship is tested (Genesis 22; Numbers 11–20). Abraham passes the test with flying colors; Israel's loyalty is still building at the end of the Pentateuch. The different endings are not incompatible, for Abraham is set up as a model while the pentateuchal drama is the ongoing story of the covenant relationship under testing.

Moreover, the role of faith in both the story of Abraham in Genesis 12–25 and the giving of the covenant in Exodus 1–24 often gets too little attention. It is clear that Abraham is constantly reiterating his trust in the promises and then the covenant offered by God, primarily in Genesis 15 and 17. But, even in Exodus, Moses and the people must affirm Yahweh's initiative and his saving power as primary to the obligations he gives to them with their assent to follow him and become his people. The scene at the burning bush in Exodus 3 and its repetition in Exodus 6, as well as the scene at the foot of Sinai in Exodus 19 and the assent of the people to the covenant in Exodus 24, all accent God's initiative and reveal no specific mutuality of status; rather God offers and they agree (Exod 19:5; 23:32; 24:7). The emphasis falls entirely on the covenant giver not on the terms of the covenant obligations.

Genesis 18:16–33, the story of how God reveals to Abraham his plan to punish Sodom and Gomorrah, uses the paired terms *mišpāṭ* with *ṣĕdāqāh* as the way in which Abraham's children are to walk ("to do *ṣĕdāqāh* and *mišpāṭ*") in verse 19, and then raises the question of God's justice (*mišpāṭ*) in punishing Sodom (v. 25), since the judge should distinguish between "the good and the evil" (*ṣaddîq* and *rešaʿ*). The assumptions presume the covenant relationship, which requires mutual *ṣĕdāqāh* and *mišpāṭ*. The use of the cognate term *šāpaṭ* for God's judging the earth generally relates to God's victory and punishment of enemies who have violated the rights of God's covenant partner Israel and defied God's obligation to watch over and protect them (see Judg 11:27; Pss 7:6–11; 17:2; 26:1–3; 28:3–4). There is a strong possibility that the related terms *mišpāṭ* and *ṣĕdāqāh* specifically refer to the maintenance of the rights of the poor and powerless under the law.

So, from this Abraham narrative, we see that righteousness is "reckoned" to a person; the idea is not legal so much as liturgical, as a priest could confer divine status on a sinner in the cult. And we also see from the drama of Sodom and Gomorrah that God is not lackadaisical or indulgent; it is the holy God, the just God who cannot tolerate unholiness, who is righteous and merciful. There is judgment:

> He is coming to judge the earth with righteousness (*ṣedeq*) and equity.
> (Ps 98:9, authors' translation)
> The LORD has established his throne for judgment (*mišpāṭ*).
> He judges the world with righteousness (*ṣedeq*);
> He judges the peoples with equity (*yōšer*). (Ps 9:7–8)

This judgment is not sheer punishment, though. God, who created the universe and all people in righteousness, is relentless in setting right what is out of sync. Since God is determined to make righteousness a reality, the people are urged to mimic that righteousness: "Thus says the Lord: Maintain justice (*mišpāṭ*), do what is right (*ṣĕdāqāh*), for soon my salvation (*yēšaʿ*) will come, and my deliverance (*ṣĕdāqāh*) be revealed" (Isa 56:1). What is the nature of this salvation and deliverance that is the restoration of lost righteousness? In other words, what is justification in the Old Testament?

4. Justification

A tragic fissure has opened between the righteousness of God and the unrighteousness of God's people. What is to be done? Although the term "justification" does not figure in Old Testament literature with anything like the centrality it assumes in the New Testament, the concept of justification has its roots in the legal procedure of ancient Israel. If an accused person is proven not guilty in court, this person is justified. This means more than acquittal; it means acceptance and reintegration into the community. Therefore, justification is never only a forensic event but always a social process. This broadens the understanding of justification considerably. We can say that the whole Old Testament is about what we may well call "justification," a making right of what has gone awry.

God, as Creator, labors to restore the harmony of creation:

> Steadfast love (*ḥesed*) and faithfulness (*'ĕmet*) will meet;
> Righteousness (*ṣedeq*) and peace will kiss each other.

The Old Testament

> Faithfulness (*'ĕmet*) will spring up from the ground,
> and righteousness (*ṣedeq*) will look down from the sky. (Ps 85:10–11)

God appears repeatedly as a savior, a deliverer. What is striking is how often justification happens with frankly nothing at all happening on the human side, no sacrifice, no repentance. Some of the most memorable passages of the Old Testament verify this habit in God's being. Ezekiel 37 casts the people of Israel as a valley of dead bones, with no capacity whatsoever to do anything at all; and yet they are joined, raised up, given life. Hosea 11 imagines a wayward people whom God simply restores because God loves; if there is any repentance, remorse, resolve, or rectification we are not privy to it. Similarly, Ezekiel 37's vision seems to enumerate absolutely no prerequisites for the divine intervention and restoration.

One of the latest and most eloquent texts, Dan 9:15–18, emphasizes the wonder of God's holy action and disposition, on which the people rely. Even as they strive to be righteous, their deep realization is that they can only abandon themselves to God's judgment, grace, and transformative power:

> And now, O Lord our God...we have sinned, we have done wickedly in view of your righteous acts (*ṣĕdāqôt*)....We do not present our supplication before you on the ground of our righteousness (*ṣĕdāqāh*), but on the ground of your great mercy (*raḥămîm*) [authors' translation].

We are reminded of a text perhaps more familiar from our liturgies, Psalm 51:

> Have mercy on me, O God, according to your steadfast love (*ḥesed*);
> according to your abundant mercy (*raḥămîm*) blot out my
> transgressions...
> Against you, you alone, I have sinned...
> so that you are justified (*tiṣdaq*) in your sentence and blameless when
> you pass judgment (*mišpāṭ*)...
> Create in me a clean heart, O God...
> Restore to me the joy of your salvation.

Clearly, for the penitent only a radical, merciful rescue on God's part, only a dramatic healing from the Lord being sought in prayer, can repair the relationship and restore *ṣĕdāqāh*. This is justification.

a. Prophetic attempts at restoration

God's concerted effort at restoration is demonstrated by the great history of prophecy in Israel. These spokesmen for God stand up not merely to castigate the people for a failure of righteousness but to declare God's righteousness and God's intention to restore a healthy relationship. Three of the most picturesque instances of *ṣĕdāqāh* in the Old Testament are found in the Minor Prophets. After an utterly failed attempt at marriage, resulting in bawdy infidelity, Hosea contends, "And I will make you my wife in *ṣedeq*, and in *mišpāṭ* and in *ḥesed* and I will marry you with *'ĕmûnāh*, that you might know that I am the Lord" (Hos 2:19–20, authors' translation). The context of a marriage relationship between God and Israel governs the first three chapters of Hosea and the combination of vocabulary in this passage stresses the goodness and faithfulness of God in his role of husband and spouse. It moves the righteousness and justice out of any legal court setting into a personal relationship between the two parties.

Amos invokes an unforgettable image: "Let *mišpāṭ* flow like water, and *ṣĕdāqāh* like a permanent stream" (Amos 5:24, authors' translation). The common pair "justice and righteousness" are placed in parallel poetic form. This normally signals that they are to be taken together as complementing one another. The context of Amos 5:21–24 is Amos's rejection of the people's liturgical and cultic observance if it is not accompanied by just actions toward other people. Perfect performance of cultic obligations for God means nothing without the perfect performance of the covenant obligations to one's neighbor.

Whereas Amos spoke primarily to the situation of the northern kingdom, and while Micah proposed a vision of a transformed Jerusalem, there are many close similarities between the two contemporaries. Both were Judean prophets from outside the Jerusalem establishment; both criticized the leadership harshly— priests, prophets, and princes alike—and both were deeply disturbed by the treatment of the poor and the weak by the upper classes. "What does the Lord require of you but to do *mišpāṭ*, love *ḥesed*, and to walk humbly with your God?" (Mic 6:8, authors' translation). There is no mention of *ṣĕdāqāh* in this passage, but "justice" is closely linked to God's mercy and the entire context mirrors Amos's condemnation of cultic perfection while the obligations to one's neighbor are neglected (see also Hos 6:6, in which cultic perfection is condemned in favor of love and knowledge of God).

We may also take note that the Emmanuel picture in Isaiah 7; 9; and 11 envisions the action of God to establish a new ruler who will deliver Judah from its enemies and reaffirm the rule of justice. But in Isa 11:4–5, it is a matter not of legal observance but of a right relationship brought about by God's "righteousness" (*ṣedeq*) and "faithfulness" (*'ĕmûnāh*). It will be exercised especially by the Davidic king, whom God will maintain forever by means of *mišpāṭ* and *ṣĕdāqāh* (Isa 9:6).

For these prophets, then, there is very little evidence of concern over the explicit performance of particular laws to be righteous. Instead, the term occurs regularly in contexts of (1) fidelity to God over other gods; (2) concern for right treatment of all groups within Israel, especially the weak or poor; and (3) trust and loyalty to the divine promise of forgiveness, salvation, and restoration.

Other prophets echo these themes. "Seek the Lord all you lowly of the land who do his *mišpāṭ*; seek *ṣĕdāqāh*; seek lowliness" (Zeph 2:3, authors' translation). "Behold, the one whose spirit is not upright in him shall fail; but the *ṣaddîq* shall live by his *'ĕmûnāh* (faithfulness)" (Hab 2:4, authors' translation). Since Hab 2:1–5 as a whole is an answer from God to Habakkuk's call for deliverance from the evil around him, the answer contrasts with the righteous, who will live because they remain faithful to God while the wicked (or crooked) will perish.

Isaiah 40–55 provides the Old Testament's most beautiful, soaring rhetoric portraying the saving righteousness of God, the "Holy One, the Creator of Israel, your King" (43:15). God is Israel's Redeemer (Isa 44:6) and Savior (Isa 45:21). Indeed, God is righteous (*ṣaddîq*) and in righteousness (*ṣĕdāqāh*) God speaks (Isa 45:21–22). God speaks the "truth" and what is "right" (Isa 45:19; *ṣedeq*). That God is "right" (*ṣaddîq*) is recognized in that God declared all that has come to pass (Isa 41:26). God acts in "righteousness" (*ṣedeq*), in accordance with the divine commitment to Israel (Isa 42:6). God's Word is trustworthy because it "has gone forth in righteousness" (*ṣĕdāqāh*), based on God's relationship with Israel (Isa 45:23).

There is another nuance which *ṣĕdāqāh* seems to have in these chapters. Most importantly, it is used to speak of divine "deliverance" (*ṣĕdāqāh*) and "salvation" (Isa 51:5, 8; also 51:6) and "vindication" (*ṣĕdāqāh*) by God (Isa 54:17; see also 58:8). God will strengthen the people with a "victorious (*ṣedeq*) right hand" (Isa 41:10). The point is that God repairs a broken relationship and corrects a situation of distress, thereby delivering and vindicating God's people. In this same vein, in the human realm, *ṣedeq* is sometimes rendered as "victor" (Isa 41:2). Human "prosperity" and "success" (*ṣĕdāqāh*) result from proper attention to the divine commandments (Isa 48:18). Humans may bring witnesses to attempt to "justify" (*yiṣdāqû*) themselves (Isa 43:9). In all of these instances, in one way or another, the point is that proper relationships will be established to the benefit of all involved. Indeed, God's "righteous (*ṣaddîq*) one, my servant, shall make many righteous (*ṣedeq*), and he shall bear their iniquities" (Isa 53:11). Clearly, *ṣĕdāqāh* is what is at stake when we find ourselves ushered into the most eloquent if mystifying, profound passages in all of Scripture.

The words of Isa 52:12–53:13 make it clear beyond doubt that God's intervention is needed to "make many righteous." Because the servant gave his life as payment for sin, "Yahweh's plan" can succeed. Because the servant bore the sins of many, because he gave his life even unto death and allowed himself to be reckoned among the sinners who had fallen away from God, because of all this, he "shall make many righteous." It is not to satisfy a higher righteousness that makes the giving of his life necessary. It is to break the ever-renewing cycle of the denial of guilt, the displacing of guilt, and the unconquered grip of sin. In taking the guilt of many on himself, the servant manages to do what otherwise the sentencing of the guilty does: he makes sin known and renders it impotent.

In what scholars agree are passages written very late in Old Testament times, the older nuances of ṣĕdāqāh continue to hold. "Behold, I shall deliver my people...and they will be my people, and I will be their god in 'ĕmet and in ṣĕdāqāh" (Zech 8:7–8, authors' translation). The close connection between 'ĕmet and ṣĕdāqāh here suggests a hendiadys: "true (or reliable) righteousness." Often 'ĕmet is paired with ḥesed (Prov 3:3; 14:22; 16:6; 20:28; Isa 16:5), with the sense of a reliable compassion from God in which we can trust. Again, as in Isaiah and elsewhere, the overall context of God's ṣĕdāqāh is his promise of salvation. Similarly, we see "Behold your king will come to you, ṣaddîq and delivering is he; humble and seated on an ass, on a colt, the son of an ass" (Zech 9:9, authors' translation). Once again, the context of God's victory over all forces arrayed against him is the central theme of this late passage. But his messiah will share in his triumph as a victor, not through glory and overbearing power, but in lowliness.

The occurrences and contexts of ṣedeq, ṣaddîq, and ṣĕdāqāh in the prophetic books are never explicitly defined as obedience to Torah commands. There are legal aspects of divine judgment in the background of nearly every passage, but the emphasis always falls on restoring the relationship between God and Israel that was broken by the people's rejection and sin, and will be restored by the ḥesed, 'ĕmûnāh, and ṣĕdāqāh of God. At this stage, the Hebrew Bible is very consistent on the salvational, covenantal, and relational settings for all uses of ṣĕdāqāh. Detection of a shift to a more forensic sense must be sought in Hellenistic contexts, the LXX, and Qumran and after.

b. Sacrifice and restoration

In these great prophetic texts, we discern the recognition that legal process cannot achieve what God ultimately desires; threat of judgment only induces fear; only divine love can accomplish what is needed—needed on the human side but also in the heart of God. On the human side, doing something is helpful, strangely essential.

It is true that Psalm 51 rather dramatically exemplifies that those who have sinned have no recourse but to cast themselves on the mercy of God; no self-justification, no moral renovation can rectify the broken relationship with God. Nevertheless, God has not cruelly, but quite graciously, provided a sacrificial apparatus so that fractured relationships with God and among people can be healed and restored. "If anyone sins against the Lord by deceiving his neighbor in deposit or through robbery, or if he has oppressed his neighbor, or found what was lost and lied about it, he shall restore what he took...and shall add a fifth to it, and give it to him to whom it belongs. He shall bring to the priest his guilt offering, a ram without blemish, valued by you...and the priest shall make atonement for him before the Lord" (Lev 6:1–7, authors' translation). In the face of guilt, two things must be done. The first is reparation; you pay back sheep for the sheep you stole.

The second we cannot actually do; it must be done for us. God's action is required. Sacramentally, a priest enacts the submission of something of value, no less than one's best. Blood must be shed, and God's power is released in that shed blood; the life of God is poured out to effect healing, to overcome that residue of guilt, the poison that haunts even the most stalwart efforts at reparation and reconciliation. Atonement is not something God is in need of; it is God's gift to his people to save them from the consequences of their sinful deeds. Atonement is *Heilsgeschehen*—God's saving act.

Forgiveness for the Israelite farmer involved real change: you parted with livestock or the fruit of the earth; they knew that there was "power in the blood," as their life labor for survival involved killing and cutting up animals; the life power ebbed out of them with the blood. What we would call reconciliation or justification was, for them, no mere spiritual or mental disposition, or any kind of inner relief from emotional pangs. Something had to be done, and a miracle ensued. Healing and grace are pardon and power: we are reunited to God, and (to borrow patristic language) made partakers in the divine nature.

c. Social justice

Our cluster of terms, both individually and used in concert with one another, *ṣĕdāqāh, 'ĕmûnāh, ḥesed, yōšer, mišpāṭ, yāšā', 'ĕmet*, and so on, all exhibit an inextricable linkage between the horizontal and the vertical, the relationship with God and the communal aspects of living faithfully. Social justice, for Israel, is not a cause, but God's blueprint for humanity, the simple outgrowth of God's creation and ownership of all that is good. This righteous God is one who is determined that there shall be a just and beneficial order of creation; if earthly kings are to ensure justice, how much more so shall the divine king seek and demand social justice? So strong is this impulse that, in Second Temple and Rabbinic Judaisms, *ṣĕdāqāh* itself came to signify "almsgiving," and the impression that the *ṣaddîq* is one who gives alms and relieves the plight of those in need.

In the Holiness Code, we read, "When you reap the harvest of your land, you shall not reap your field to its very border; you shall not strip your vineyard bare, neither shall you gather the fallen grapes of your vineyard. You shall leave them for the poor and for the sojourner. I am the Lord your God" (Lev 19:9–10, authors' translation). The crop has finally matured, my family is hungry, the year has proven to be lean, I am exhausted but excited—and I am not to reap all I have labored for all these months? To leave the grapes I accidentally dropped, to leave desperately needed grain ungathered, are physically embodied reenactments of what we can only call grace.

If our theological construals of grace, or reconciliation, or justification understand the spiritual transaction involved as entirely one-sided, as a gift God gives to those who have not merited any good gift, then the reaping of a field can become not merely a visual illustration of what God is like but a real-life implementation of the grace of God. Who gets the grain and grapes? Really, just anybody who is hungry. God's goodness is not to be hoarded, but spread around, made available for free to strangers. The average Israelite had to do something so as not to squander the covenant; or the Israelites together had to engage in certain practices so as not to jar the lovely order of the cosmos established in grace by Yahweh. This graceful enactment of *ṣĕdāqāh, 'ĕmûnāh, ḥesed, yāšār, mišpāṭ, yēšaʻ,* and *'ĕmet* illustrates the way what God is after is relational—a responsible relationship with God that gets on board with God's projects, and hence that righteousness is relational among the haves, have-nots, and thus everyone on earth.

5. Summary of Salient Points in the Old Testament

In the introduction, we said that Christians reading the Old Testament will learn much and come to understand much about righteousness. The story and identity of *ṣĕdāqāh* in the Old Testament are complex and intriguing, providing significant background to New Testament and Christian construals of justification. A cluster of terms and set of realities, as comprehensive as all of life, come into play when we think of righteousness, which is, primarily and always, something that is in God. But God shares; God disburses righteousness to the people, and yearns for them to embody that which begins in God's mind and heart.

Not surprisingly, the people succeed at times and falter more often. Their very ability to achieve some measure of righteousness becomes the prickliest aspect of their failure: when they become "righteous in their own eyes," they locate themselves at some distance from God. Yet God is gracious; God provides the mediators and mechanisms that the people need to be justified, either in the sense of receiving the divine stamp of approval for their righteousness in the face of false accusations or evildoers, or in the sense of sinners in need of mercy and restoration to the presence of God and the life of the community.

So, righteousness may seem like some absolute standard, some pillar of the nature of God, a legal corpus to be enforced. But the mood of righteousness in the Old Testament is always relational, as God quite personally pursues the best conceivable relationship with the people as a whole and each individual in the community; and, since the people bear an immense responsibility and the joyful privilege of living together in a special way, that echoes the very nature of God. So reconciliation is always the order of the day, and social justice is incumbent upon all who have discerned the righteous character and actions of God. A special bias presses Israel to be hospitable and kind to the marginalized—the stranger, the widow and the orphan, and the one who seems hopelessly in the wrong. For to enact this proclivity toward the one who cannot demand or expect justice is to mimic what God has done for the people who realize in humility that they have no recourse but to entrust themselves entirely to the judgment and mercy of God.

We can see various threads coming together that together form the fabric of thought that helped explain the startling story of Christ in the New Testament. A meaningful relationship with God is a wonderful but imperiled reality. It requires both demand and yet immense patience on God's side, and a receptive openness on ours, the shedding of pride and the gaping astonishment over the possibilities of the reconciled life. Jesus Christ is not mentioned once in the Old Testament; but the resonances of his being and God's enactment of the unfailing covenant of grace echo through its pages, especially when *ṣĕdāqāh* and its kindred terms are in play. We need not be surprised by the way in which the diverse but jointly lifted voices of the New Testament articulate their witness to the Christ event based on what we know—even if they define a richer fulfillment, and even if they seem inattentive to a few items on the menu of righteousness in the Old Testament.

6. Early Jewish Reception

Referring to biblical ideas about God's righteousness, Paul and other New Testament authors are part of the lively process of the reception of Israel's Scriptures. The Septuagint, in particular, and nonbiblical early Jewish literature attest to the existence of this dynamic. For the New Testament authors as well as for the authors of these Jewish writings, "Scripture" was not simply a text coming from a distant past. The *Tanach*, the three-part collection of Jewish Scriptures consisting of the Torah, the Prophets, and the "Writings," was received as God's Word for the present. Translations from Hebrew into Greek (the Septuagint) or Aramaic (the Targums) were also understood in this way.

a. Hellenistic context

New Testament authors used the Greek language to express their beliefs and their theological convictions. They employed Israel's Scriptures in Greek translation to express the rootedness of the gospel in the religious traditions of Israel. Although some of them were able to go back to the earlier Hebrew or Aramaic wording of the biblical texts, the translation of Hebrew or Aramaic writings into Greek necessarily caused changes in meaning of biblical terminology and biblical concepts. Thus, the biblical message of God's righteousness in God's dealing with Israel as expressed in several texts of the Hebrew Bible was received by the authors of the New Testament in a form shaped by its use in early Judaism.

As can be seen from the Qumran manuscripts, the wording, contents, and order of the writings that Christians would later call the Old Testament were still not definitively established by the time that the New Testament writings began to make their appearance. Nevertheless, the authors of the New Testament were able to refer to "the Scripture(s)" explicitly and implicitly. When they wanted to express or explain the gospel, the New Testament writers were able to quote from the

Scriptures verbatim. Therefore, the New Testament writings are to be seen within the history of reception and interpretation of Israel's Scriptures in early Judaism.

Because of its theological concepts as well as its methods of interpretation of Scripture, early Christianity is linked with early Judaism even if it is separated from it by its confession of Jesus Christ. The use of the Old Testament in the New Testament shows that for the first Christians the Christ event could be appropriately described only on the basis of a belief in the salvific actions of God on behalf of Israel similar to that of contemporary Jewish believers.

There are, obviously, distinctions between the biblical understanding of God's righteousness expressed in the Hebrew writings of the Old Testament and the philosophical and ethical notions of justice in the Greek philosophical tradition. The use of the terminology for God's righteousness in the Septuagint is, however, much more determined by its biblical contents than it is by Greek philosophical concepts. In this respect, the Septuagint's understanding of God's righteousness is similar to that of most other Jewish writings of the time. Within the context of the reception of the Hebrew Scriptures, it must be said that there is no fundamental difference between the Hebrew Bible and the Septuagint with regard to the understanding of God's righteousness.

b. Early Judaism

An important change in the understanding of righteousness in early Judaism came about with the association of the idea of righteousness with the Torah. The Torah was understood as God's salvific gift and a pattern of life for his people. God's covenant with Israel is to be seen as an expression of his righteousness. That Israel was required to keep God's commandments is part of the covenant relationship between God and Israel. In early Judaism there was a tendency to emphasize a connection between God's righteousness and eschatological consummation and judgment. At the end of time, God will show his righteousness toward Israel by punishing those who violate the commandments of the Torah. At the same time, God will manifest his mercy and forgiveness, which are greater than his wrath.

These ideas belong to Jewish religious convictions about God; they are not restricted to the Christian belief about God. The *Book of Jubilees*, for example, links together the giving of the Torah to Moses on Mount Sinai, a revelatory speech of God about Israel's future sins, an announcement of the judgment against Israel because of its violation of the Torah, and an expression of Israel's repentance, to which God will react with mercy. "I shall reveal to them an abundance of peace in righteousness. And with all my heart and with all my soul I shall transplant them as a righteous plant....And I shall not forsake them and I shall not be alienated from them because I am the Lord their God" (*Jub.* 1:15–18).[1] When Moses asks God not to abandon his people and to keep them from departing from the "ways of righteousness," he receives this promise: "I know their contrariness and their thoughts and their stubbornness...I shall create for them a holy spirit, and I shall purify them so that they will not turn away from following me from that day and forever....And they all will be called 'sons of the living God'...that they are my sons and I am their father in uprightness and righteousness. And I shall love them" (*Jub.* 1:22–25).

In early Judaism there is no opposition between keeping the commandments of the Torah and trust in the merciful God. This can be seen, for example, in the ending of Qumran's so-called *Halakhic Letter*. The following exhortation is directed to the letter's addressee:

> Remember David, one of the "pious" and he, too, was freed from many afflictions and was forgiven. And also we have written to you some of the works of the Torah which we think are good for you and for your people, for we saw that you have intellect and knowledge of the Law. Reflect on all these matters and seek from him that he may support your counsel and keep far from you the evil scheming and the counsel of Belial, so that at the end of time, you may rejoice in finding that some of our words are true. And it shall be reckoned to you as justice when you do what is upright and good before him, for your good and that of Israel. (4QMMT 398, frg. 14–17 II)[2]

Prayers of repentance in the Book of Daniel as well as in several Qumran texts and the *Apocalypse of Ezra* (*Fourth Ezra*) provide impressive evidence that in early Judaism God's righteousness is an expression of his salvific will. The one who prays turns to God with the request:

> O Lord, in view of all your righteous acts (LXX: *tēn dikaiosynēn sou*), let your anger and wrath, we pray, turn away from your city Jerusalem, your holy mountain; because of our sins and the iniquities of our ancestors, Jerusalem and your people have become a disgrace among all our neighbors....Open your eyes and look at our desolation and the city that bears your name. We do not present our supplication before you on the ground of our righteousness, but on the ground of your great mercies. (Dan 9:16–18)

A prayer in Qumran's *Rule of the Community* reads:

> As for me, if I stumble, the mercies of God shall be my salvation always; and if I fall in the sin of the flesh, in the justice of God, which endures eternally, shall my judgment be; if my distress commences, he will free my soul from the pit and make my steps steady on the path; he will draw me near in his mercies, and by kindness set in motion my judgment; he will judge me in the justice of his truth, and in his plentiful goodness always atone for all my sins; in his justice he will cleanse me from the uncleanness of the human being and from the sin of the sons of man, so that I can give God thanks for his justice and The Highest for his majesty. (1QS XI 11–15)

Qumran's *Hymns* show an awareness that sin can only be entrusted to God's righteousness:

> What is flesh compared to this [God's glory]? What creature of clay can do wonders? He is in iniquity from his maternal womb, and in guilt of unfaithfulness right to old age. But I know that justice does not belong to man nor to a son of Adam a perfect path. To God Most High belong all the acts of justice, and the path of man is not secure except by the spirit which God creates for him to perfect the path of the sons of Adam so that all his creatures come to know the strength of his power and the abundance of his compassion with all the sons of his approval....I thought, for my offences I have been barred from your covenant. But when I remembered the strength of your hand and the abundance of your compassion I remained resolute and stood up; my spirit kept firmly in place in the face of affliction. For I leaned on your kindness and the abundance of your compassion. For you atone iniquity and cleanse man of his guilt through your justice. (1QH XII 29–37)

In *Fourth Ezra* the sinner tellingly reflects about his experiences of sin. Although he knows that those who keep God's commandments will obtain life, he has come to know that there is almost no one who meets this demand: "For who among the living is there that has not sinned, or who among man has not transgressed your covenant?" (*4 Ezra* 7:46; trans. Bruce M. Metzger). "For all who have been born are involved in iniquities, and are full of sins and burdened with transgressions" (*4 Ezra* 7:68). "For in truth there is no one among those who have been born who has not acted wickedly, and among those who have existed there is no one who has not transgressed. For in this, O Lord, your righteousness and goodness will be declared, when you are merciful to those who have no store of good works" (*4 Ezra* 8:35).

This selection of references from early Jewish sources about trust in God's righteousness shows that New Testament authors were linked with an understanding of God that was thoroughly coined by traditions of belief from Israel as collected and transmitted in the biblical writings. But, whereas in early Jewish tradition trust in God's righteousness was linked with the requirement to keep the Torah, in the New Testament this biblical understanding of God was newly and eschatologically defined by the Christ event.

7. Key New Testament Passages in the Old Testament Context

New Testament writers read the texts of the biblical Scriptures as people of their time, and most of them as people who lived within the tradition of early Judaism. But, at the same time, their encounter with Christ gave them a new perspective for understanding Scripture and led them to highlight some passages that had become crucial for this understanding.

From a New Testament perspective, there are three key Old Testament passages on the biblical theology of justification.

- In Romans (Rom 4:3, 9) and Galatians (Gal 3:6) Paul quotes Gen 15:6 as scriptural evidence of the message of justification; the Letter of James (Jas 2:23) also refers to it when dealing with justification.
- Further, Paul quotes Hab 2:4 in Romans (Rom 1:17) and Galatians (Gal 3:11) as scriptural evidence of justification by faith; Hebrews takes up the same verse in 10:38 to support the exhortation to have faith (Heb 10:32–39) but does not explicitly relate it to the doctrine of justification.
- Paul twice quotes Isa 28:16 in Romans to support the theology of justification (Rom 9:33; 10:11), and the First Epistle of Peter also cites this verse in connection with the image of the cornerstone to explain the church as a communion of faith. The parallel text in Isa 7:9[3] is not taken up explicitly in the New Testament.

There is no close connection between these verses in the Old Testament. They do not relate to each other systematically until Paul, in particular, refers to them in the New Testament. There are differences between the original Old Testament meaning and the New Testament understanding of the texts. These differences are important for biblical theology; the ecumenical movement may well make use of them.

The Old Testament verses cited in the New Testament to underpin the theology of justification are quoted also in contemporary Judaism, but that is a different context for understanding (reception); the passages thus take on other meanings, even respecting the basic concept of "faith." We will give a brief description of these differences and reflect on them hermeneutically.

a. Genesis 15:6

Genesis 15:6 relates to a covenant (Gen 15:1–23) sealing the promise to Abraham (Gen 12:1–3). The whole thing starts with Abram's complaint that he has no direct descendants. His lack of offspring calls the validity of the promise into question. After God repeats the promise (Gen 15:1), Abram laments his fate to God (Gen 15:2–3), prompting a more specific promise (Gen 15:4–5). Then follows the key sentence of the narrator, who in Jewish and Christian tradition is identified with Moses: "And he believed the Lord...."

What is meant by "belief" here is a matter of dispute already in the domain of biblical tradition. Judaism takes a prospective view. Abraham's faith is regarded as one that proves itself at the time of trial, particularly in the "Binding of Isaac" (Genesis 22), and in his obedience to the law, starting with circumcision (Genesis

17). That is the interpretation of the Letter of James, which seeks to prove that faith and works belong together according to the example of Abraham, albeit bypassing circumcision and emphasizing the readiness to sacrifice Isaac (Jas 2:21–24).

Paul, by contrast, takes a retrospective view, in which he is not alone. The Jewish philosopher Philo of Alexandria points to the role of conversion (*De Virtutibus* 211–19; *De Praemiis et Poenis* 27). However, Paul sees Abraham's faith as consisting in his trust in the validity of God's promise. Romans 4 covers the situation of childlessness described in Genesis 15, with Paul using it to highlight the faith of Abraham as belief in the God who "gives life to the dead" (Rom 4:17).

The subject of the second part of the sentence (Gen 15:6) is not absolutely clear in the Hebrew. However, for the Septuagint, the whole of Jewish tradition, and the New Testament, the subject of the sentence is God. The Hebrew is then to be translated: "...and the Lord reckoned it to him as righteousness." In the Greek versions found in the New Testament, the sentence is in the passive, in order to stress that God is the subject: "Therefore his faith 'was reckoned to him as righteousness.'"

In Gen 15:6, righteousness in the broadest sense means keeping the covenant in Abraham's relationship to God, from which flows blessing for the people. This fundamental meaning of righteousness is deeply rooted in the Hebrew Bible. It is preserved in the early Jewish and New Testament quotations, even if Christology brings about differences in ways of understanding the covenant and the realization of God's desire for universal salvation. The early Jewish sources also agree with the New Testament writings that it is faith that justifies, even if understandings of faith diverge.

God "reckons" Abraham's faith to him as righteousness. We can also translate that as God "recognizes his faith." Neither the Hebrew Bible, the Septuagint, nor early Jewish and early Christian interpretations understand this as a settling up on the principle of service and return of service. God is the subject; God passes judgment, creating righteousness. The Hebrew word *ḥāšab* is partly derived from sacred law in which God declares profane things to be sacred and partly from the salvific oracle in which God makes a promise on which one can rely. Either way, what is meant is God's creative word. The "reckoning" relates to the faith inspired by God, assigning it the infinitely great value it has in God's eyes. The Greek word *logizein* comes from the world of business and may stress the process of either bookkeeping or settling up. The logic is the same: faith is recognized by God and given infinitely more value. God notes the nature of the faith called forth by divine righteousness, thereby creating what alone can lead to the fulfillment of the promise: Abraham's righteousness.

b. Habakkuk 2:4

In the Hebrew text, Hab 2:4 speaks of the faith of the righteous: "The righteous live by their faith"—or "their faithfulness," another possible translation.

That is the climax of a promise of salvation that God makes to the prophet Habakkuk for the whole people (Hab 2:1–4), after having lamented the misery of Israel (Hab 1:12–17) and before enumerating at length all possible risks of missing out on the promise (Hab 2:5–20). Life means rescue from present distress. The translation of the Hebrew word ('ĕmûnāh) as "faithfulness" focuses on the fact that the righteous consistently live by God's Word. In Qumran the verse is related to the future of those who rely entirely on the understanding and consistent practice of the law. It "concerns all observing the Law in the House of Judah, whom God will free from the house of judgment on account of their toil and their loyalty to the Teacher of Righteousness" (1QpHab 8:1–3).[4] One could equally render the Hebrew term 'ĕmûnāh as "faith," indicating the tense situation in which Habakkuk receives the promise of rescue; faith is then the trust that God does everything well, although in human eyes everything points to the contrary. The Septuagint, by contrast, relates "faithfulness" (*pistis*) to God and thereby underlines that those who are righteous can gain life through God alone.

Quoting the prophet in Greek, Paul again gets closer to the meaning of the Hebrew text in speaking of people's faith. He interprets the situation at that time of threat to Israel in terms of the threatening and fatal power of sin, from which only God can save. Exegetes disagree on how to translate his quotation: "The one who is righteous by faith will live"[5] or "The one who is righteous will live by faith" (Rom 1:17). In the first case, Paul would have read Hab 2:4 ("But the righteous live by their faith") as a direct proof of his justification theory and, in the second case, as indirect proof.

c. Isaiah 28:16

Isaiah 28:16 is part of the warning of coming judgment, with which the prophet criticizes disloyal priests and prophets in Jerusalem (Isa 28:7–15). They have been lulled into false security, believing that they can rely on the promises of God and the election of Zion, which, however, they betray through their corruption. So God speaks through the mouth of the prophet: "See, I am laying in Zion a foundation stone, a tested stone, a precious cornerstone, a sure foundation: 'One who trusts will not panic.'" In the Book of Isaiah this gives a positive turn to the prophet's warning to King Ahaz: "If you do not stand firm in faith, you will not stand at all" (Isa 7:9). Isaiah 28 prophesies a worldwide judgment by God, who makes "justice the line and righteousness the plummet" (Isa 28:17).

In both the Hebrew original and the Greek translation of Isa 28:16, faith means being grounded in God. It is trust in God's promise that is connected to the practice of law and justice, because it is God who creates law and justice. Only through this faith will the people of God enjoy a safe tomorrow.

In Rom 9:33, Paul connects Isa 28:16 with Isa 8:14 and thus sharpens the prophetic criticism: the cornerstone that holds the whole house together is a "stumbling block." The image in the First Letter of Peter is similar (2:6–7) and links the quotation from Isa 28:16 with a reference to Ps 118:22: "The stone that the builders rejected has become the chief cornerstone" (Mark 12:10; Matt 21:12; Luke 20:17; Acts 4:11). In the context of Romans and Pauline theology, there can be no doubt that the apostle Paul—like the author of 1 Peter—is thinking of the crucified and risen Christ. This preaching about Christ is what causes most Jews to reject God's gospel in their "zeal for God" (Rom 10:2). But this rejection does not stop God from affirming the divine promises (2 Cor 1:20). While in the middle of reflecting about how Israel's election relates to the universality of mission and how the hardening of hearts relates to the final salvation of Israel, Paul focuses on the good news, which he has been sent to proclaim, quoting the plain promise of salvation (for the second time): "No one who believes in him will be put to shame" (Rom 10:11; see Rom 9:33).

d. Evaluation

Contemporary methods of Bible exegesis allow us to link up Old Testament statements and New Testament quotations and to recognize better their theological significance from the perspective of the Judaism of the time.

The Old Testament positions are constitutive for Paul and the author of James, who explicitly point to statements in Israel's Bible about faith and righteousness in their teachings on justification. The quotations are important to back up their argument. However, the life, death, and resurrection of Jesus have created a new standpoint in the New Testament, from which the Old Testament texts are read in a new light. Faith is given a new quality through confessing Christ, righteousness through the justification of the baptized, the fulfillment of the law through love, and the promise of the covenant through the calling of the nations.

The Old Testament statements do not lose their significance for the Christian doctrine of justification through the christological interpretations in the New Testament. Exegetical discernment opens up new horizons. The Old Testament is a fundamental part of Scripture, even seen from a New Testament perspective. From the original Old Testament texts it becomes clear that no doctrine of justification may bypass the lasting election of Israel and the validity of the law. Any doctrine of justification in accordance with the Scriptures (*secundum scripturas*) is founded on faith as an elementary trust in God that finds its genuine place in the people of God. The New Testament quotations from the Old Testament adduced to justify the doctrine of justification exemplify how we can deepen ecumenical understanding through the hermeneutic of Jewish–Christian dialogue.

V

The New Testament

1. Introduction

The New Testament is the collection of the apostolic witness to Jesus Christ and to all that God has done through him. Coming from different apostolic traditions in early Christianity, the writings within the New Testament proclaim and teach different aspects of the gospel of Jesus Christ. At a first glance, the doctrine of justification by faith alone seems to be represented by only a small sector of New Testament writings. Even in the writings of Paul, only the letters to the Galatians, the Philippians, and the Romans deal in a more detailed way with this matter.

This leads to the question of whether, if we consider the teaching of the New Testament as a whole, it is appropriate to give the doctrine of justification as prominent a place as it has in the theology of the Reformers and is agreed upon by Lutherans, Methodists, and Roman Catholics in the *Joint Declaration on the Doctrine of Justification.*

In order to answer this question, the New Testament section of our study will take as its starting point the writings of Paul (section 2) in order to explore the meaning and importance of the theology of justification. Without question, this is the key element of the biblical theology of justification as well as the point of reference for most of its interpretations during its reception history.

We will also look to those traditions in the New Testament that testify to Jesus' ministry and the saving act of his death and resurrection (section 3). From a biblical or "canonical" perspective, this is the basis for the whole of the church's message. The Gospels and sometimes even the letters of the New Testament collected and transmitted what was remembered and retold of Jesus' sayings and stories. We refer to these traditions of Jesus' proclamation as "the gospel of Jesus Christ" and will ask whether or not we can find in it the roots of a theology of justification.

Finally, we will examine other important theological concepts within the New Testament that are often seen as contradictory to the (Pauline) theology of justification (sections 4–6). Do they really represent opposing or even contradictory models, or are they rather alternative forms of expressing the grace of God, as revealed in the gospel of Jesus Christ, which underline the basic meaning of the theology of justification without using its terminology? With this question in mind, we shall, in the first instance, turn to the Gospel of Matthew as a narrative representation of the gospel of Jesus Christ, which develops the relationship between Jesus' proclamation of the kingdom of God, the law as the expression of God's will, and justice as the eschatological fulfillment of God's saving acts to humankind. The Gospel of John expresses a similar intention through several theological concepts or linguistic means, which, while differing from Paul's as well as Matthew's, point in the same direction. Even the Letter of James, often seen as being contradictory to the Pauline message of justification, can be read as a testimony to God's grace and to human actions as the consequence of faith in the gospel of Jesus Christ.

2. The Theology of Justification in Paul

The prominence of Paul's theology of justification in ecumenical church documents

The church's doctrine of justification bears the decisive imprint of Pauline theology. Reaching a common agreement on a joint ecumenical reading of Paul that is appropriate to the message and the influence of his theology, while also being able to withstand the scrutiny of Pauline research, will be of great importance for deciding whether the differentiated consensus on the doctrine of justification has a sufficiently solid biblical basis.

The status and understanding of Pauline theology
in the ecumenical movement

In the past, interdenominational controversies about justification commonly revolved around Paul; in our day, he has been discovered as an ecumenical figure, not only with regard to the doctrine of justification but also with regard to such subjects as baptism, the Eucharist, and ministry. Pauline theology is at the basis of an ecumenism that does not gloss over differences but bears with differentiated consensus. The "truth of the gospel" (Gal 2:4, 15)—which according to Paul is at stake in the matter of justification by faith—requires different modes of testimony based on a solid common foundation in order to be more clearly recognized in all its richness.

In the American study *Justification by Faith* (1983), and the German study, *Lehrverurteilungen—kirchentrennend?* (1986), as well as in the international studies *The Gospel and the Church* (1972) and *Church and Justification* (1994), the apostle Paul's doctrine of justification has been examined in detail and used to achieve a differentiated consensus. The problem raised during the Reformation period and the historical consequences of this problem dominate all the studies that preceded the *JDDJ*—the document refers to this problem and its consequences throughout—but the pertinence of Pauline theology is at the basis of these studies. All of them benefit from the results of ecumenical Pauline research conducted intensively throughout the second half of the twentieth century.

One of the hermeneutical accomplishments of these studies is the methodological differentiation between the constellation of problems in the sixteenth century and those of the New Testament period. Differences between Paul and Luther are identified, as are differences between Paul and the Council of Trent. Drawing attention to these differences is not intended to call into question the legitimacy of the Reformation or of the Tridentine doctrines of justification; rather, their aims are the following:

First, to clarify the respective significance and continuing relevance of both the Lutheran and the Tridentine positions, which are indeed different but not contradictory when one takes into account their starting points, their structure, and their intention.

Second, to explore the possibility of clarifying the meaning of Scripture, in particular the Pauline witness, beginning with its meaning in its original context, and then using it to develop church doctrine within a context of ecumenical partnership.

Paul's theology of justification as reflected in the Joint Declaration on the Doctrine of Justification

Pauline theology enjoys a preeminent position in the *JDDJ*'s description of the biblical basis of the doctrine of justification (*JDDJ*, 8–12). Because of the comprehensive preliminary studies to which the *JDDJ* refers throughout, chapter 1 (paras. 8–12), "Biblical Message of Justification," was intentionally brief. With special attention to the Letter to the Romans (*JDDJ*, 9) the Declaration explains how the apostle proclaims "the righteousness of God is revealed through faith for faith" (Rom 1:17) and understands "justification" as the salvific event (Rom 3:21–31). The christological foundation of justification is presented as clearly as the understanding of faith, the basis of the doctrine in Scripture as clearly as the efficacy of justification.

In addition to the paragraph on the witness of Scripture, Pauline theology is—explicitly and implicitly—present in the *JDDJ* wherever the fundamental commonalities in the doctrine of justification are described (*JDDJ*, 14–18), on the one hand, and, on the other, wherever the existing differences are stated and evaluated in such a way that they do not appear as church dividing but rather as forming an ecumenical bond. This is as true of the definitions of the relationship between sin and human responsibility (*JDDJ*, 19–21) and the relationship between imputing righteousness and making righteous, as it is of the relationship between faith and grace (*JDDJ*, 25–27) and the relationship between law and gospel (*JDDJ*, 31–33). Even old points of controversy, such as the notion of *simul justus et peccator* (*JDDJ*, 28–30), the certainty of salvation (*JDDJ*, 34–36), and good works (*JDDJ*, 37–39), are considered in an ecumenical analysis of Pauline theology in such a way that a nuanced consensus is apparent.

With regard to the theological crux of the ecumenical doctrine of justification, the *JDDJ* states in the form of a confession of faith that "justification is the work of the triune God....Together we confess: By grace alone, in faith in Christ's saving work and not because of any merit on our part, we are accepted by God and receive the Holy Spirit, who renews our hearts while equipping and calling us to good works" (*JDDJ*, 15).[1] This interpretation reprises a reading that was current in the sixteenth century and remains quite relevant today. It is our task to define the foundation, the goal, and the substance of the doctrine of justification in Paul within a broader horizon and develop it ecumenically.

In the Annex to the Official Common Statement both sides explicitly agree that no church teaching may contradict the criterion of the doctrine of justification. Nevertheless, some Catholic voices assert that they are unaware that the antithesis between faith and the works of the law does any such thing in their tradition. There are also Lutheran critics who are of the opinion that the significance of the doctrine of justification as the article by which the church stands or falls (*articulus stantis et cadentis ecclesiae*) is understated in the *JDDJ*. At this point, exegesis must determine the status of the doctrine of justification for the apostle Paul himself and compare that with its reception in tradition in order to arrive at a well-founded judgment for today. Furthermore, it must evaluate it with regard to its ecumenical ramifications.

The discussion of Paul's theology of justification in recent exegesis

Pauline research has developed considerably since the nineteenth century. This development is the result not only of an interest to identify the contemporary relevance of the doctrine of justification but also of new studies on Paul, early Judaism, the Old Testament, and other traditions in the New Testament. At this point, it is not possible to do anything more than briefly indicate how the current state of research has developed and what theological perspectives have thereby been opened up. Ecumenical theology relies on further research on Paul without becoming dependent on any particular trend in research.

a. The anthropological interpretation of the message of justification in the twentieth century: the model of personal achievement

Twentieth-century Catholic and Lutheran Pauline research was shaped by growing ecumenical collaboration. Fruitful partnerships were able to develop after the papal encyclicals *Providentissimus Deus* (1893) and *Divino Afflante*

Spiritu (1943), and the Second Vatican Council freed Catholic biblical studies from restrictive regulations.

The *Leistungsprinzip* (achievement principle) has been crucial in terms of the interest in the interpretation of the Pauline doctrine of justification in the twentieth century, especially in Germany. The focus was on anthropology. The destruction of the notion of religious achievement appeared to be the critical point of the doctrine of justification. Paul rejected the validity of the human attempt to justify oneself before God because of one's religious works.

Twentieth-century ecumenical theology was strongly influenced by this interpretive trend, which allowed for a new presentation of the interpretation of Paul not only by Luther but also by the Council of Trent, which also stressed the idea of human salvation.

b. A new understanding of the early Jewish context of Pauline theology

In the last third of the twentieth century, new developments in Pauline research were greatly enriched by ecumenical theology, which opened up three new possibilities:

- Combining the ecumenical understanding of the theology of justification with a renewed relationship between Christianity and Judaism
- Exploring the anthropological focus of the theology of justification with regard to the ecclesial and missionary dimension of faith
- Establishing a connection between the theology of justification and recent political and social debates on justice and participation

An essential stimulus comes from a new view of Judaism and its significance for Pauline theology.

On the one hand, the consideration and evaluation of old and new sources have changed the picture of early Judaism. Important texts from the time of Jesus and the apostles show that Judaism is not a "religion of personal achievement." These texts testify to the justification of sinners through God's grace.

On the other hand, much greater attention has been paid to the Jewish roots of Paul and Pauline theology. Paul did not renounce Judaism because of his calling and "conversion." Rather, he came to a new understanding of the witness of Scripture and of the fulfillment of the law.

Recognizing the Old Testament roots of Christianity and of Paul, determining precisely the commonalities and differences between Christian thought on justification and Judaism, and connecting the mystery of the salvation of Israel (Rom 11:26) with the justified person's hope for salvation (Rom 5:1–11) are therefore intrinsic to an ecumenical theology of justification.

Studying the *Sitz im Leben* (setting in life) of the theology of justification provided further impetus for the development of Pauline exegesis with regard to justification. Its fundamental soteriological significance cannot be called into question. There has been considerable research on the role of circumcision and the works of the law in Judaism. These "identity markers" served to distinguish the people of God from the Gentiles. Moreover, it has been emphasized that the Pauline doctrine of justification received its form and its importance because of the mission to the Gentiles and the struggle for the unity of a church consisting of Jewish and Gentile Christians. It is therefore integral to the task of an ecumenical theology of justification to grasp and articulate the ecclesial and social dimensions of Pauline theology.

c. The critique of salvation theology by political and cultural models of interpretation

Some sectors of exegetical research have cast doubts on the coherence of Pauline justification theology, but in turn they have also been criticized. As a result of this debate, ecumenical theology has been put on guard against erecting a closed system of justification theology; it must remain constantly focused on the witness of Scripture and measure itself against the yardstick of Pauline theology, which, intrinsically, is many layered.

Other research has inquired further into a theologically focused interpretation of Paul and has worked through the social and political implications and interests of justification theology. Impetus deriving from this research's critique of ideology can help ecumenism to make concrete the message of justification while helping it to study the theological content of justification within past and present political, cultural, and social contexts, and highlighting its intended and its current effects.

d. Searching for a new model of ecumenical exegesis: Participation in Christ through faith

The critique of notions of religious achievement remains one of the essential tasks of an ecumenical theology of justification. The relevance of Martin Luther's criticism of "works," intended to impress God as religious achievements, remains undiminished. How human beings act in order to do good and to avoid evil cannot save them. Salvation, which has been promised, is infinitely greater than any human merit. The result of sin, while small in relation to grace (Rom 5:12–21), is far greater than the human capacity to overcome it.

Recent Pauline research shows that the apostle linked the grace of justification with participation in God's love and with the community of believers that emerges from that love. Thus, there has been increasing ecumenical consensus on the significance of the model of participation.[2] In our ecumenical study we are not subject to any particular exegetical school of thought; rather, our aim is to benefit from the critique of the exegetical basis of the doctrine of justification found in the *JDDJ* and to offer an interpretation of Paul within a broader perspective.

Salvation theology in the Letters of Paul that do not have a justification-centered soteriology

The theology of justification is central to the Letters to the Galatians, the Philippians, and the Romans. Paul can, however, proclaim the gospel and speak of God's grace without making explicit reference to the justification of those who believe. He does so in several of his letters. Rather than diminishing the importance of the theology of justification, this difference demonstrates the breadth of Pauline theology. This is of great importance for ecumenism.[3]

a. First Thessalonians: The theology of election

The First Letter to the Thessalonians, presumably the earliest of the apostle's writings preserved in the New Testament, bears witness to the missionary proclamation of the faith to the Gentiles. The Gentiles are called into the kingdom of God (1 Thess 2:12). Hence, they find a place within the church (*ekklēsia*).

Although neither "righteousness" nor "justification" is mentioned in the letter, 1 Thessalonians is a characteristic document of Paul's proclamation of salvation and has important ecumenical implications. In this letter, Paul emphatically speaks about faith as well as love and hope, about the imitation of Christ, the redemption of the faithful and God's wrathful judgment, the future resurrection from the dead, and perfect communion with Jesus Christ. Paul emphasizes sanctification (1 Thess 4:1–8) and proclaims the eschatological fulfillment of salvation: "God has destined us not for wrath but for obtaining salvation through our Lord Jesus Christ, who died for us, so that whether we are awake or asleep we may live with him" (1 Thess 5:9–10).

b. First Corinthians: The theology of the cross and resurrection

The First Letter to the Corinthians is a major witness to Paul's theology of the cross and resurrection. This theology is linked to a theology of faith and grace, sanctification and communion with Christ, baptism and the Eucharist. It is developed without any explicit theology of justification, but in no way does it contradict the theology of justification expressed in the Letters to the Romans, the Galatians, and the Philippians; in fact, it concurs with the doctrine of justification.

The First Letter to the Corinthians mentions righteousness only once: "He is the source of your life in Christ Jesus, whom God made our wisdom and our righteousness and sanctification and redemption" (1 Cor 1:30). This verse comprehensively defines what being Christian means. The verse proclaims Christ as the reconciler who, as the crucified one (1 Cor 1:8–24), embodies the wisdom of God and is therefore the one who sanctifies and redeems humankind, by allowing God's righteousness to become theirs. Likewise, justification is mentioned only once in the First Letter to the Corinthians. In a manner similar to that of 1 Cor 1:30, Paul says to the Corinthians: "You were sanctified, you were justified in the name of the Lord Jesus Christ and by the Spirit of our God" (1 Cor 6:11).

This letter also speaks about the law. Paul sees his freedom as an apostle to be related to his missionary engagement. This leads him to be "to the Jews...as a Jew," but to "those outside the law...as one outside the law," although, of course, "under Christ's law" (1 Cor 9:20–21). In the chapter on the resurrection (1 Corinthians 15), Paul writes: "The sting of death is sin, and the power of sin is the law" (1 Cor 15:56). His dense wording presupposes reflection on the fatal power of sin and the law's domination by means of sin.

In 1 Corinthians, Paul reflects on faith as a formative power that shapes the whole of life. Nonetheless, he develops the understanding of faith not in contrast to works of the law, but in contrast to the wisdom of the world (chs. 1–2) and boasting based on self-reliant strength (ch. 4). Yet the theology of Christ's death and resurrection, which Paul develops pneumatologically in the Letter to the Galatians (ch. 3) and in the Letter to the Romans (6:1–11), forms part of the christological basis of the doctrine of justification.

c. Second Corinthians: The theology of redemption

The Second Letter to the Corinthians also lacks a developed doctrine of justification. Nonetheless, Paul writes about God and God's action in Christ: "...he made him to be sin who knew no sin, so that in him we might become the righteousness of God" (2 Cor 5:21). The apostle speaks of Christ's taking the place of sinners, up to his death, because he identifies with them out of love, so that "in him" they become participants in God's righteousness. While this is the core idea of the message of justification, in 2 Corinthians Paul develops the idea not by means of the antithesis between faith and the works of the law, but within the horizon of a theology of reconciliation (2 Cor 5:11–21). In the Letter to the Romans, Paul explicitly links reconciliation to the theology of justification (ch. 5).

In 2 Corinthians 3–4, Paul develops the relationship and the difference between law and gospel. These chapters are particularly important for ecumenism. They are relevant not only for the relationship between Lutherans and Catholics but also for the relationship between Jews and Christians. According to Paul, both the law and the gospel convey God's glory, the first in Moses' ministry, the second in the apostle's ministry. Both have been established by God. The crucial difference between the two is that the law condemns sin and conveys death, while the gospel sets the sinner free through Jesus Christ. This dialectical critique of the law corresponds exactly to the doctrine of justification. In 2 Corinthians 3–4, the apostle's focus is, however, on developing the meaning of the apostolic ministry within the parameters of God's eschatological work of salvation. In turn, this is oriented to the participation of the faithful in God's salvation, in which they partake through the proclamation of the gospel. Whoever faithfully acknowledges Jesus as Lord reflects the glory of God (2 Cor 4:4–6).

Conclusion

Paul cannot proclaim his theology without dealing with the creative grace of God, communion with Christ, the working of the Holy Spirit, saving faith, and a criticism of human boasting, but he can and does do so without explicitly developing a theology of the justification of those who believe.

Highlighting the breadth of theological motifs and the wealth of theological language in Paul does not by itself respond to the issue of the particular importance and substance of the theology of justification. Rather, the theological language of Paul's letters offers two elements for ecumenism:

In examining the theology of different church traditions, even when one applies Pauline standards, it is a matter not so much of whether the language of justification is present as of the substance of the theology of justification being expressed. There are many possibilities of drawing from the great reservoir of Pauline theology without playing off one way of speaking against another. Ecumenical theology offers exegesis an outstanding opportunity to discover the breadth of Paul's theology of grace and faith—theology in dialogue.

In the theology of the different denominations, the important thing is whether each in its own way retains the critical and constructive function of the explicit theology of justification. In this, Pauline exegesis plays a key role. In dialogue with exegesis, ecumenical theology has an outstanding opportunity to lay the foundation for a differentiated assessment that strengthens unity in faith.

The setting of Paul's theology of justification

The apostle's theology of justification reflects the experience and praxis of faith in the church, the missionary call, and the struggle for communion. At its core, Paul's theology of justification is an exposition of the Christ event. In discourse about God and the work of salvation, the theology of justification functions as a criterion because it distinguishes between truth and error, hypocrisy and authenticity.

The theology of justification develops its criteriological significance in extremely important constellations and conflicts. Three typical constellations can be identified briefly:

- The human cry for redemption
- The mission to Jews and Gentiles
- The unity and communion of the church

a. The need for salvation

"Wretched man that I am! Who will rescue me from this body of death?" (Rom 7:24). This question is posed by Paul and answered by his message of the justification of the believer.

Paul highlights the human need for salvation. His theology of justification emphasizes the deadly power of sin. Even Jews, to whom the law has been given, must confess their transgressions. Gentiles have the voice of conscience but repeatedly fail to follow it (Romans 2). Even seemingly trivial wrongs reveal the fundamental sin of covetousness. Paul cites the commandment from the Decalogue (Rom 7:7; cf. Exod 20:17; Deut 5:21) and relates it to Adam's sin, his disobedience against God (Gen 3:5; cf. Rom 5:12–21). Only God can conquer the death that is caused by sin.

Paul proclaims the possibility and the reality of salvation by faith. God is merciful; God has sent Jesus Christ as savior. This is affirmed in faith. The theology of justification fulfills its criteriological function in both its critique of trusting in salvation by means of the law and its orientation of the totality of one's life by means of the fruits of the spirit (Gal 5:22–23).

b. The mission

In the Letter to the Galatians, Paul defends and outlines the message of justification in the face of criticism coming from opponents who maintained that uncircumcised Gentiles could not be members of the people of God (ch. 2). According to Luke, a similar scenario lies behind the Apostolic Council in Jerusalem. Pharisees who have become Christians claim, "It is necessary for them to be circumcised and ordered to keep the law of Moses" (Acts 15:5). Paul has to address this criticism not only to assure the effectiveness of the mission to the Gentiles but also to do justice to the fundamental salvific significance of the Christ event and membership in the body of Christ (1 Cor 12:12–13). With its fully developed theology of justification, the Letter to the Romans offers a theological program for the mission to the Gentiles (Rom 1:8–17; 15:14–29). Paul's idea that it is not the works of the law but rather faith in Jesus Christ that justifies lays the foundation for the mission to the Gentiles. In this way the message of justification stands in the service of God's will for universal salvation.

At the Apostolic Council (cf. Gal 2:1–10; Acts 15), the criteriological significance of the theology of justification is acknowledged and given prominence by the church of Jerusalem. Luke specifically mentions the apostles and presbyters there; Paul names, in particular, the three acknowledged pillars: James, Cephas (Peter), and John. Justification theology is not compatible with the position of Paul's opponents, who, in addition to faith, require works of the law, especially circumcision. According to Paul and also Luke, albeit with a rather different emphasis, the legitimacy of mission to the Gentiles was recognized because the working of the Spirit could be seen in it. According to Luke, the so-called James clauses (Acts 15:19–20, 28–29) do not contravene this principle. These clauses, with implicit reference to Leviticus 17–18 and with Jewish parallels, prescribe minimal rules for the sake of unity with Jewish Christians.

c. The struggle for communion

According to Paul, the Apostolic Council not only laid the foundation for the freedom of the mission to the Gentiles (Gal 2:4) but also sealed the communion (*koinōnia*) of the apostles with handshakes. This shaking of hands has become the most important symbol of the ecumenical movement. It is based on a fundamental consensus about the gospel, which, with regard to its practical significance for faith, is safeguarded by means of the message of justification.

Apostolic *koinōnia* is grounded on *koinōnia* with Jesus Christ (cf. 1 Cor 10:16–17). Because it is based on communion with Christ, the communion of the apostles is based on faith and the praxis inherent in it. By the same token, any substantial disagreement with regard to the theology of justification is an unmistakable sign that the relationship with Jesus Christ, the one *Kyrios*, has been disturbed.

Apostolic *koinōnia* does not mean uniformity. Paul describes two different basic kinds of mission: one to the Jews, the other to the Gentiles (Gal 2:9). This diversity of mission does not divide the church; rather, it reveals the breadth of faith, the difference of praxis, and the capacity to acknowledge others and their mission on the basis of the theology of justification.

Following his description of the Apostolic Council, Paul reports on his conflict with Peter, Barnabas, and other Jewish Christians in Antioch (Gal 2:11–14). After James's intervention, they withdrew from the common table with Gentile Christians. Eucharistic communion was probably also affected by this action. Paul accuses Peter of hypocrisy because, in his description of the Apostolic Council, Paul reports concerning his conflict with Peter, Barnabas, and all the other Jewish Christians in Antioch that they were "not acting consistently with the truth of the gospel" (Gal 2:14). Paul's criticism is based on his understanding that it is not the works of the law that justify but rather faith in Jesus Christ (Gal 2:15–16). For Paul, the aim of the dispute is to bring about not division but unity. Accordingly, Paul formulates the justification thesis in the first person plural from a Jewish Christian standpoint. He appeals to the knowledge of faith that Peter should by rights share but has ignored in this situation. From Paul's point of view, confirmed by the canon of Scripture, the theology of justification proves itself in situations of conflict. It provides the foundation for the unity of Jewish and Gentile Christians in the church. This is not a specifically Pauline teaching but the apostles' basic and shared insight regarding the truth of the gospel. Nonetheless, this truth must be recognized again and again, even in situations of conflict.

Basic Pauline texts for the theology of justification

In the Letters to the Romans, the Galatians, and the Philippians, Paul explicitly and antithetically formulates the theology of justification by faith. In these texts, the core of justification theology becomes evident. Their content and context reveal what the explicit theology of justification consists in, and how and where it differs from other equally essential expressions of faith.

The theology of justification is Paul's soteriological interpretation of the Christ event. For the apostle, it is essential to show that the message of justification by faith is rooted in Scripture. Genesis 15:6 (cf. Rom 4:3, 9, 22; Gal 3:6), Hab 2:4 (Rom 1:17; Gal 3:11), and Isa 28:16 (Rom 9:33; 10:11) are the most important scriptural texts because they connect faith and justification. Nevertheless, it is not only these proof texts that are important; the theology of justification is based on the entire witness of Scripture. In his reflection on the law and works, sin and redemption, faith and love, Paul always refers back to Moses and the prophets. In the Pauline letters, the quotations from Scripture are real arguments, not mere embellishments.

It is obvious that Paul reads Scripture from a christological perspective. It is also clear that he understands Scripture in a particular way. It is Scripture, the Old Testament, as a whole that provides the theological basis for his argumentation.

The basic texts for the theology of justification, presented below in their canonical order, form part of a dense network of theological motifs, ideas, and statements that closely link the Letters to the Romans, the Galatians, and the Philippians with the remaining Pauline letters and other traditions in the New Testament. They indicate the place and context of statements about justification in Paul.

a. Romans 3:28 and parallels

The thesis of the Letter to the Romans is that in the gospel God's righteousness is revealed as the power that saves all who believe (Rom 1:16–17). After writing about God's just wrath with regard to the sins of both Jews and Gentiles (Rom 1:18–3:20), the apostle grounds the justification of believers in Christ's expiatory death for them (Rom 3:21–26). From the christological salvific event he deduces the salvific effect of faith: "We hold that a person is justified by faith apart from works prescribed by the law" (Rom 3:28). This is followed by an argument that makes reference to the principal commandment of the Old Testament (Deut 6:4–5): If God is the one God, then God is not only the God of the Jews but also the God of Gentiles. God cannot establish different standards of justification; one standard suffices for everyone: justification comes not through works of the law but through faith (Rom 3:27–31).

In his translation of Rom 3:28, Martin Luther introduced the word "alone": without works of the law, through faith alone. The addition expresses Luther's interpretation of justification in the sense of *sola fide*, which is consistent with the apostle's intention. Hence, according to the *JDDJ*, *sola* (alone), as an expression of the common understanding of justification by faith, is acceptable within

Catholic theology. The faith that "alone" justifies is faith working through love (Gal 5:6).

Later, in his Letter to the Romans, Paul refers back to this basic affirmation several times:

Paul writes with respect to Abraham, "But to one who without works trusts him who justifies the ungodly, such faith is reckoned as righteousness" (Rom 4:5; cf. Rom 4:13, 16). Similarly, with regard to David, Paul writes, "…God reckons righteousness apart from works" (Rom 4:6). In a concluding observation, Paul applies the story of Abraham to all believers: "Now the words 'it was reckoned to him' were written not for his sake alone, but for ours also" (Rom 4:23–24).

In the chapters on Israel (Romans 9–11), Paul writes about election, "not by works but by his call" (Rom 9:12). Paul says about Christians, "For one believes with the heart and so is justified, and one confesses with the mouth and so is saved" (Rom 10:10; cf. 11:16).

The antithesis between one's own righteousness and "God's righteousness" (Rom 10:3; Phil 3:9) as well as the antithesis between "works righteousness" and "righteousness through faith" (Rom 9:32; cf. 9:30–31; 10:5–6) are part of the explanation of Rom 3:28.

b. Galatians 2:15-16

In the Letter to the Galatians, Paul links the fundamental thesis of justification by faith with his account of the Antiochian conflict. He expresses the theology of justification for the sake of the "truth of the gospel" from which Peter has deviated (Gal 2:14). He bases the "freedom" of faith—his response to the criticism of the mission to the Gentiles—on this theology that refers to faith and baptism rather than to circumcision and works of the law. Paul uses the first person plural in order to show the Galatians that with regard to the theology of justification there is no disagreement between him and Peter, only consensus: "We ourselves are Jews by birth and not Gentile sinners; yet we know that a person is justified not by the works of the law but through faith in Jesus Christ.…because no one will be justified by the works of the law" (Gal 2:15–16). This conclusion recalls Ps 143:2 and thus emphasizes that for Paul the message of justification is in accord with the witness of Scripture.

Throughout the letter, Paul develops the theology of justification by means of various arguments. These demonstrate that theologically the message of justification is based on Christ's salvific death "for us" (Gal 3:13–14). They express the spirit-filled salvific effect of faith (Gal 3:1–18), offer a definition of the theological meaning of the law (Gal 3:19–25), and clarify the praxis of faith in love (Gal 5:6). In the Letter to the Galatians, the expression of the theology of justification has a polemical thrust. Consequently, the personal, missionary, and ecclesial implications of the message of justification are sharply focused.

c. Philippians 3:4–11

In the Letter to the Philippians, Paul affirms:

> If anyone else has reason to be confident in the flesh, I have more: circumcised on the eighth day, a member of the people of Israel, of the tribe of Benjamin, a Hebrew born of Hebrews; as to the law, a Pharisee; as to zeal, a persecutor of the church; as to righteousness under the law, blameless. Yet whatever gains I had, these I have come to regard as loss because of Christ. More than that, I regard everything as loss because of the surpassing value of knowing Christ Jesus my Lord. For his sake I have suffered the loss of all things, and I regard them as rubbish, in order that I may gain Christ and be found in him, not having a righteousness of my own that comes from the law, but one that comes through faith in Christ, the righteousness from God based on faith. (Phil 3:4–9)

In Philippians 3 Paul links the truth of the message of justification with his call to be an apostle and his conversion from being a violent persecutor of Christians to become a preacher of the gospel. Knowing Christ Jesus is the decisive factor (Phil 3:9–10); it is knowledge in faith that follows from the revelation of Jesus Christ (cf. Gal 1:13–16). Justification leads to a fundamentally new understanding of the righteousness of God and one's own righteousness. Justification does not come through the law, even though Paul can claim to have led a life of blameless obedience to God's commands. God's saving righteousness originates in faith in Christ, one that leads to communion with Jesus Christ, to life formed by the death and resurrection of Christ.

Justification as the salvation event in Paul

Justification is the event of redemption, perfected in the future but already determining the present. Its dimensions are accurately indicated by the explicit formulations and contextual development of the theology of justification in Paul's letters.

In light of recent Pauline research, we can consider that in principle the issue of whether or not a forensic or performative understanding of justification dominates Paul's thought has been overcome:

Judgment holds a place of great importance in the justification event. All hope is directed toward being acquitted by God. Nonetheless, what is promised for the last judgment determines the present also, since the Word of God has creative power.

The reality of justification comes from God alone, God's will and Word. Justification occurs at the present time on the basis of faith in anticipation of acquittal in the eschatological judgment.

a. God's justice or righteousness and the justification of those who believe

In the Letter to the Romans, Paul develops the theology of justification as a theology of God's righteousness or justice. It is generally agreed that this divine "righteousness" or "justice" of which Paul speaks is not something that God demands from human beings but something that God demonstrates to men and women insofar as he justifies them. This was Luther's new discovery in his interpretation of Rom 1:16–17. In principle, a similar conviction is found also in Augustine and Aquinas. The conviction was likewise expressed at the Council of Trent.

According to Paul, God's faithfulness to his promises is clearly an essential trait of divine righteousness. "God is faithful" (1 Cor 1:9; 10:13; 2 Cor 1:18; 1 Thess 5:24; cf. 2 Thess 3:3). God stands by his word. God fulfills his promises. In his theology of justification, Paul, especially in two ways, concretely expresses this fundamental theological principle, which is deeply rooted in the witness of the entire Scripture:

Through Jesus Christ (Rom 15:8), God fulfills the promise made to Abraham to be a blessing for all nations insofar as God justifies those who believe—both Jews and Gentiles—just as Abraham's faith was reckoned to him as righteousness (Gen 15:6; see Rom 4:3, 9, 22; Gal 3:6; cf. Jas 2:23).

In Romans 9–11, the chapters about Israel, Paul writes, "The gifts and the calling of God are irrevocable" (Rom 11:29). Therefore, there are grounds for hoping for the salvation of all Israel (Rom 11:26).

God's faithfulness to his promises is precisely because God is dependable and reveals the truth to humankind.

It is debatable whether God also lets justice prevail in the sense that God gives to each person what that person deserves and would seem to contradict God's grace and forgiveness of sins. The good news consists precisely in the fact that sinners and the ungodly are justified through faith. Nevertheless, Paul speaks about God's wrath and judgment. In Rom 1:18–3:20, Paul argues that "the wrath of God is revealed from heaven against all ungodliness and wickedness of those who by their wickedness suppress the truth" (Rom 1:18). The wrath of God is God's reaction to human sin, but it is overcome by God's righteousness (Rom 1:16–17; 3:21–26). Therefore, the day of judgment is part of the gospel proclaimed by Paul (Rom 2:5–16). While Romans 2 considers Jews and Gentiles, other Pauline texts clearly have Christians in mind. Justified by faith, all believers will "stand before the judgment seat of God" to give an account of themselves to God (Rom 14:10–12; cf. 2 Cor 5:10). They must render account of their deeds and wait for reward or punishment. They are, nonetheless, full of hope because of God's promise (1 Cor 3:12–15; 1 Cor 4:4–5; also Rom 12:19; cf. Deut 32:35). This judgment does not annul God's grace (Rom 8:1–2). According to Paul, the grace of God is proof of the justice of God:

- Because Jesus Christ takes on himself—in their stead—the verdict that condemns sinners to death (Rom 3:21–26).
- Because human beings, freed from the alienation of sin because of the justification event, come to themselves, as the image of God, as the beloved brothers and sisters of Jesus Christ (Rom 8:28–31).

b. Justification by the grace of God

"[T]hey are now justified by his grace as a gift through the redemption that is in Christ Jesus," Paul writes about sinners at the theological core of the Letter to the Romans (Rom 3:24). In Galatians, in the conclusion to his first argumentation for the theology of justification's antithesis between faith in Christ and the works of the law, Paul says, "I do not nullify the grace of God; for if justification comes through the law, then Christ died for nothing" (Gal 2:21).

Paul emphasizes God's grace for various reasons:

- No one has a claim on justification and salvation because of the magnitude of guilt and the overflowing greatness of salvation, only God can be the savior.
- In the justification of the believer, God does not act arbitrarily; rather, in justifying those who believe, God fulfills the divine plan of salvation. The divine plan of salvation is defined by God's unfailing love toward humankind, even when humans behave as the enemies of God. In love God turns to humankind and grants men and women the gift of salvation. This is the core of the grace of God.

In Rom 5:12–21, Paul develops a qualitative mismatch between guilt and grace with regard to Adam and Christ. As evil as human sin may be, God's grace is incomparably greater. It is a new creation (Gal 6:15; cf. 2 Cor 5:17). Justification constitutes a real renewal of the human being, brought about by the Spirit of God (cf. Rom 7:1–6).

There is an intrinsic connection between justification by faith and justification by grace. In Romans 4, the chapter on Abraham, Paul formulates this principle: "For this reason it depends on faith, in order that the promise may rest on grace..." (Rom 4:16). He explains the reverse of the principle in Rom 11:6, "But if it is by grace, it is no longer on the basis of works, otherwise grace would no longer be grace" (cf. Rom 4:4). Since sin cannot be undone nor guilt totally assuaged and no one is able to resist the fatal power of sin, it is by pure grace that God justifies the sinner on the basis of faith. The principle of grace is given its preeminence precisely because it is faith, rather than works of the law, that justifies. When Paul speaks about reward, he adds "by grace" in order to exclude any notion that God repays according to human standards and to include the idea that God promises eternal life.

His theology of grace moves Paul to speak of "cooperation" by human beings. This problematic issue in the ecumenical dialogue is discussed in detail in the *JDDJ*. In Paul it is clear that God's action does not need supplementary human action in order for salvation to be achieved. God alone acts through grace in justification. Through grace, the action, the responsibility, the faith of humankind are included, not excluded. Through justification, human beings are freed. Hence, "with" is an important preposition in Paul's theology of justification.

What God does "with" the believer through Jesus is fundamental. In baptism those who believe are "buried with" Christ "into his death" (Rom 6:3–4) and are "crucified with him" (Rom 6:6) in order to "live with him" (Rom 6:8; cf. Rom 9:7). The "for us" of God and Jesus Christ takes place in this "with" (Rom 8:31–39). "With" primarily refers to the future culmination of salvation (1 Thess 5:9–10), but proleptically it also refers to present salvation.

What the faithful do "with" God derives from that which God fundamentally and continually does "with" them through Christ. One example is Paul's apostolic ministry (1 Cor 3:9; 15:10; 2 Cor 6:1). Another is the action of the congregation gathered in the power of the Spirit (1 Cor 5:4).

Harking back to Paul's theology of grace reveals the basis for criticism of those models of cooperation that amount to a moralization of salvation. Recalling Paul's theology of grace also reveals grounds for the thinking that so strongly emphasizes the grace of God and that God draws human beings into his salvific act.

c. Justification in Christ

Just as justification is grounded in God's grace, so it takes place "in Christ" (Rom 3:24; Gal 2:17; 5:6; cf. Rom 6:11, 13; 8:1–2, 39; Gal 2:4; 3:26–28; 6:15). "Being in Christ" is a leitmotif of Pauline theology; it is also to be found in those letters that do not explicitly develop a theology of justification. For Paul, to be "in Christ" is not only to be justified "for the sake of Christ" but also to be in a living relationship of faith with Jesus Christ, shaped by his love. "In Christ" highlights the fact that the justification that Paul proclaims is not an external process; rather, it is a salvific event that transforms an entire person from within with the love of God bestowed upon that person through Jesus Christ.

In Galatians, Paul bases his entire faith experience on the love of Jesus Christ. "I have been crucified with Christ; and it is no longer I who live, but it is Christ who lives in me. And the life I now live in the flesh I live by faith in the Son of God, who loved me and gave himself for me" (Gal 2:19–20). In Romans, Paul sees an intrinsic unity between the love of God and the love of Jesus Christ that leads to the justification of the believers and their hope for salvation (Rom 8:31–39). In Rom 5:1–11, he links God's love of his enemies with the reality that Jesus, his Son, whom God has given "for us" died "for us" "while we were still weak… [and] ungodly" (Rom 5:6). By the resurrection of Jesus from the dead, this love became not only something of the past but also an abiding reality in the present. With the same love with which Jesus gave his life for the justification of the faithful (cf. Rom 4:23–24), he intercedes "for" them at the right hand of God. All who believe are in Christ because Christ and the Spirit are in them (Rom 8:11–12).

d. Justification and baptism

Both the Letter to the Galatians and the Letter to the Romans refer to baptism in the context of the theology of justification (Gal 3:26–28; Rom 6:1–11). For Paul, the justification of those who believe and the salvific effect of baptism are not antithetical. Between them there is an intrinsic connection. Faith leads to baptism and is nourished by it. Baptism mediates the grace of God through faith.

The ecclesial character of the event of justification is found in the link between justification and baptism. On the one hand, baptism is forgiveness of sins as well as incorporation into the body of the church (1 Cor 12:13–27) and unification with Christ. On the other, baptism replaces circumcision as the sacrament of initiation. The antithesis between faith and works of the law is directed against the requirement of circumcision, whose consequence would be an obligation fully to observe the law (Gal 5:3).

e. Justification and new life in the Spirit

The Holy Spirit inspires and motivates believers to live as those who have been justified in the communion of the church, and to witness to the word of God in their lives. Peace with God is a fruit of the Spirit (Rom 8:6). In the Spirit, the love of God is poured out into the hearts of believers (Rom 5:5). Believers live as people whom God has reconciled to himself (2 Cor 5:17–21).

The justification of believers implies their adoption as children of God. "You are all children of God through faith" (Gal 3:26), for there is only one baptism for Jews and Gentiles, slaves and free, men and women (Gal 3:27–28). For Paul, adoption as children of God includes two related aspects:

Whoever is a child of God is not a slave but free. That person has a claim to the inheritance, participation in the promises (Gal 3:26—4:7). Whoever is a child of God has Jesus Christ as brother and is conformed to his image (Rom 8:29). The Spirit teaches the faithful to call God "Abba" (Gal 4:6; Rom 8:15) and, as children of God, to love God as their father.

The believers' claim of citizenship "in heaven" which they enjoy already in the *ekklēsia* is grounded in election by God (Phil 3:20). The theology of justification links participation in the people of God not with circumcision but with faith and baptism. The right to codetermination and participation is inherent to citizenship. In this sense, the doctrine of justification possesses considerable force, both within and outside the church.

Justification is freedom. In Galatians Paul writes, "For freedom Christ has set us free" (Gal 5:1). A few verses later, he expresses the idea in this way: "For you were called to freedom" (Gal 5:13). These statements enjoy the same status as other expressions of Jesus' salvific effectiveness (Gal 1:4; 3:13–14; etc.). They draw out the consequences of the doctrine of justification. The Letter to the Romans likewise contains strong statements pertaining to the freedom of believers.

Freedom is defined both negatively and positively:

- Negatively, freedom is freedom from sin and, consequently, from death insofar as death is the "wages of sin" (Rom 6:23). Freedom from the law belongs to this context insofar as the law does not justify human beings but rather condemns them as sinners (Rom 7:1–6).
- Positively, freedom is freedom to love, showing itself in service of one's neighbor, which is derived from God's service (Gal 5:19–23).

Both dimensions are determined by faith insofar as faith bears the promise of forgiveness and fosters the service of justice through participation in the life of Christ (Rom 6:13–14). Faith has the power to free because it leads to the eradication of self-alienation (Rom 7:7–24) and to discovery of the "I," which is determined by the love of Jesus Christ in the Spirit (Gal 2:19–20).

Paul links justification to sanctification. This connection is expressed not only in brief phrases in 1 Corinthians (1 Cor 1:30; 6:11) but also in the developed arguments of the Letter to the Romans: "But now that you have been freed from sin and enslaved to God, the advantage you get is sanctification. The end is eternal life" (Rom 6:22; cf. 6:19). The sanctification of life is imparted and shaped by God's will in the Holy Spirit.

Justification and sanctification belong together, however, because justification is directed toward a life of righteousness in which faith becomes concrete. Sanctification of life is based on the liberation from sin, accomplished through justification and baptism (Rom 6:1–14). Justification and sanctification differ insofar as Paul develops the idea of justification in the context of conversion and the genesis of faith, while, when speaking about sanctification, he directs his attention to leading a Christian life.

The service of righteousness is an aspect of the justification of believers. A just way of life is not a prerequisite for justifying grace; rather, faith in the power of the Spirit shapes life according to God's will. Paul had to deal with an accusation that his theology of grace lessens moral responsibility (Rom 6:1, 15; cf. Gal 2:17). Paul does not respond to this by relativizing God's creative grace; rather, he emphasizes the link between the righteousness of God and the righteousness of human beings. Justifying grace leads to communion with Jesus Christ, who does not share in Adam's disobedience but who lives and dies entirely in obedience to God (Rom 5:12–21). Therefore, whoever believes is led by Jesus Christ into the service of righteousness (Rom 6:11–14).

f. The struggle between flesh and spirit

In his Letter to the Galatians, Paul deals with issues deriving from believers' new life in Christ (Gal 5:16–25). In Gal 5:16, he exhorts his readers to "live by the Spirit." Again, in Gal 5:25, he writes, "If we live by the Spirit, let us also be guided by the Spirit." In the entire passage, Gal 5:16–25, Paul reflects on the importance of this exhortation and on the hope that God's grace will lead believers to live in accordance with the gospel.

In the course of his argument, Paul observes that the desire (*epithymia*) of the flesh continues to exist and struggles against the spirit (Gal 5:16–17). In Rom 7:7, in which Paul quotes the commandment "You shall not covet" (*ouk epithymēseis*) of Exod 20:17 and Deut 5:21, the desire is sin, which is condemned by the law (cf. Rom 13:9). In Galatians 5, the "desire of the flesh" is a kind of persecution that is dangerous for believers. This persecution happens in the "flesh" of believers. Writing in regard to nonbaptized Jews and Gentiles in Rom 1:24, Paul says, "God gave them up in the lusts (*epithymiai*) of their hearts to impurity."

The believers' "flesh" is weak, but "God has sent the Spirit of his Son into our hearts, crying, 'Abba! Father!'" (Gal 4:6). However strong the desire of the flesh may be, the power of the Spirit is greater. Believers should, nonetheless, be aware of the power of sin, which leads to works of the flesh (Gal 5:19–21). Because believers are not "subject to the law," but are "led by the Spirit" (Gal 5:18), they are able to produce "the fruit of the Spirit" (Gal 5:22–23).

The old controversy—part of the discussion of the *simul justus et peccator* formula—as to whether desire (*epithymia, concupiscientia*) lies at the root of every sin or provides an incentive to sin (*fomes peccati*) is at a different level from the Pauline discussions in Galatians 5 and Romans 7 or the discussions in other New Testament texts (1 John 1–2; see below). In light of Paul's anthropology and soteriology, we must affirm what is declared in the "Annex of the Common Official Statement" (2A), namely, that there is a "persisting danger that comes from the power of sin and its action in Christians. To this extent Lutherans and Catholics can together understand the Christian as *simul justus et peccator*, despite their different approaches to this subject as expressed in JD 29-30."

g. Justification and hope for salvation

Justification through faith is the foundation of the hope for final salvation, as Paul writes to the Galatians, "For through the Spirit, by faith, we eagerly wait for the hope of righteousness" (Gal 5:5).

In Paul, hope is not an uncertain presentiment, as it was among Greeks. Rather, it is a firm expectation shaped by two factors:

- Knowledge that fulfillment, seeing God, is yet to come; in the meantime, we, together with all creation, suffer from the powers of sin and death (Rom 8:20–28).
- The revelation of God's righteousness in Jesus' death and resurrection which has once and for all brought about salvation (Rom 6:10).

Hope directs those who are justified in faith toward future eschatological fulfillment. It links them with those who suffer injustice. It accords with a confession of faith in the resurrection of Jesus from the dead.

The exclusion of the works of the law in Paul's theology of justification

A major debate in Pauline research is the understanding of the phrase "works of the law." This topic, a key issue in ecumenical theology, is also promising for promoting the rapprochement between Christian and Jews. It is undeniable that over a long period of time both Catholic and Protestant interpretations of Paul, specifically with reference to Paul's theology of justification, have represented Judaism as a legalistic religion claiming to be in the right, a view of Judaism against which Christianity has sought to define itself as a morally more significant religion. Any ecumenically focused appreciation of the theology of justification must criticize and overcome this view.

The question of the validity of the law is linked with the discussion of the works of the law. What meaning does the law have within the divine plan of salvation? What is the relationship between Paul's criticism of the law, especially in the Letter to the Galatians, and the fulfillment of the law, which Paul links with justification by faith in Galatians and Romans? These two questions have traditionally provided points for controversy between Catholics and Protestants. With a different emphasis, they continue to be controversial in contemporary Pauline research.

a. Contemporary scholarly controversy

The idea that Paul excluded the "works of the law" from justification because these works were seen as achievements that substantiated claims made before God has, previously and often, been considered a legitimate criticism against Judaism. Today, in contrast, Paul is criticized as having presented a caricature of Judaism in his theology of justification and thus having fostered anti-Judaism. Both points of view need to be critically examined.

A number of recent studies interpret the exclusion of the works of the law in sociological rather than anthropological terms. According to these studies, for Paul the phrase "works of the law" does not mean all the commandments of the law but only circumcision and regulations pertaining to diet and ritual purity. At the time of Second Temple Judaism, these precepts served as identity markers to maintain the identity of the Jewish people and to distinguish them from Gentiles. Hence, it is often concluded that Paul's criticism of the works of the law was directed against the conditions governing entrance into the faith community of the church, rather than life within that community to be lived in conformity with the law. Other interpretations of Paul highlight differences between Jewish and

Christian identity constructions. Ecumenical study has to take this research into consideration.

b. Perspectives for an understanding of the works of the law

The social dimensions of the works of the law form part of the missionary and ecclesial *Sitz im Leben* of the theology of justification. These social dimensions do not, however, negate the anthropological dimensions because, for Paul, membership in the church is an essential marker of the identity of those who are justified. The church is nothing other than the communion of the faithful.

Circumcision is a crucial link between Paul's theology of justification and his critique of the works of the law insofar as circumcision is viewed as a necessary condition for affiliation with the church. Dietary regulations and rules of ritual purity are likewise connectors insofar as they are seen as obligations incumbent on both Jewish and Gentile Christians. Paul, however, also applies his criticism to general principles, linking criticism of the works of the law with a theology of the law that defines the divine determination of the law in christological terms.

In the Judaism of Paul's era, "works of the law" can mean prescriptions and regulations of the Torah (4QMMT). But in Galatians 3 and Romans 4, Paul discusses deeds that a human being, with God's help, can do by following the law in obedience to God's will. "Works of the law" are regulations *and* actions determined and demanded by the law. They provide evidence of fidelity to the law and membership in God's people, Israel.

c. The reason for excluding works of the law from justification

The reason for excluding the works of the law from justification in Paul is based on his understanding of the law. Before his Damascus experience, Paul was a Pharisee convinced that the holiness of God demanded complete fulfillment of the law as the way to salvation. Because of the revelation granted to him (Gal 1:16), Paul came to recognize this view as erroneous. Jesus Christ rather than the law mediates the grace of justification and salvation.

Nevertheless, this critique of the law does not lead Paul to devalue the law, but rather to discover its holiness anew: "So the law is holy, and the commandment is holy and just and good" (Rom 7:12).

d. Works of the law and the curse of the law

The law presents Israel with the alternatives of blessing or curse (Deut 30:15–20). In the Letter to the Romans, Paul states that there is no person who keeps the entire law (Rom 3:1–20). Consequently, all human beings stand under the curse of the law (Gal 3:10). Paul bases this idea on Scripture: "Cursed be anyone who does not uphold the words of this law by observing them" (Deut 27:26, cited in Gal 3:10).

According to Paul, the curse that the law pronounces upon the sinner is integral to its holiness. God's righteousness punishes the sinner. The fatal power of sin is expressed and directed back to its perpetrator in the curse of the law.

It is not the law that frees humans from the "curse of the law"; rather, it is Jesus Christ alone who took the curse of the law upon himself in the stead of all sinners: "Christ redeemed us from the curse of the law by becoming a curse for us—for it is written, 'Cursed is everyone who hangs on a tree'—in order that in Christ Jesus the blessing of Abraham might come to the Gentiles, so that we might receive the promise of the Spirit through faith" (Gal 3:13–14). Justification occurs not because the curse of the law is invalid or ineffective but because Jesus Christ, who is without sin (cf. 2 Cor 5:21), takes the curse on himself, so that the sinner is freed from the curse and is able to participate in the blessing of Abraham.

"Works of the law" do not have the power to overcome the "curse" of the law because transgressions of the law always occur, no matter how many or how few they may be. Works of the law cannot compensate for the deadly effect of the transgressions of the law.

e. Works of the law and the power of sin

For Paul, the fact that the "works of the law" cannot lead human beings to escape the "curse" of the law depends on the superior power of sin. The law has been given by God in order to create life (Lev 18:5; cf. Gal 3:12; Rom 10:5). But, since the fall of Adam, the law cannot display its power for life in such a way that human beings can be justified by "works of the law." According to Gal 3:19–25 and Rom 5:20, the law was proclaimed to make sin manifest as sin and to afflict sinners with the consequences of their actions as transgressors.

For Paul, sin, which cannot be conquered by the law but only by Jesus Christ, is not merely a transgression of the law, despite the fact that each offense against God's commandments is a sin (Rom 2:17–29). Rather, sin is a deadly power that, since Adam's fall (Rom 5:21), encumbers human life. Sin cannot be overcome by humans, only by God. Paul develops this concept of sin by means of an apocalyptic intensification of the wisdom tradition's link between acts and their consequences. No one can excuse their sins by saying that others also sin, or that sin exerts a coercive power that results in temptation and seduction. The power of sin derives new energy from every misdeed, every transgression of the law, and every offense against the law of love.

The catastrophic power of sin is the catastrophic power of death. On the one hand, it is true that "the wages of sin is death" (Rom 6:23) because sin curtails life. On the other hand, "the sting of death is sin" (1 Cor 15:56) because death destroys human life insofar as it drives men and women to sin.

Deliverance from the power of sin is accomplished through deliverance from the power of death, which takes place in the future eschatological fulfillment in the resurrection of the dead (1 Cor 15:20–28). Eschatologically it takes place in the present through faith and baptism because there the "I" of the sinner is crucified with Jesus Christ, who gave his life for humankind so that men and women might live life anew in the power of the resurrection of Jesus Christ (Gal 2:19–20; Rom 6:4–5).

In Rom 7:7–25, Paul analyzes the power of sin over the law. From early times, this has been a controversial text both exegetically and, in recent centuries, for disputes among Christian traditions. Dispute centers on the three ways to identify the "I" in the passage:

- As the "I" of Paul who is reappraising his Pharisaic past
- As the "I" of the believer who ponders the reality of constant temptation by sin, the weakness of flesh, and desire
- As the "I" of Adam who describes his temptation by God's command and his alienation under the law.

Luther, like Augustine, understood the "I" to be the "I" of the believer. This debate about the "I" has had considerable importance in the discussion of *simul justus et peccator,* since Romans 7 is a significant, if not the only, scriptural proof text for the view espoused in this formula.[4]

The three understandings of "I" show why Paul deems that the law cannot prevail against the power of sin.

The commandment itself leads to transgression because human beings, subject to sin, convince themselves that they are improving life through desire, at the cost of others (Rom 7:7–12).

With the help of the law, sin deceives human beings (Rom 7:11), either by provoking transgression by reason of the law, or by fostering the error that humans can be justified by the "works of the law."

Through sin, the law contributes to the alienation of human beings from themselves (Rom 7:15–20). Persons of flesh are "sold into slavery under sin" by the law which sin misuses (Rom 7:14).

Humans who are subject to sin and know only the law can only cry for help: "Wretched man that I am! Who will rescue me from this body of death?" (Rom 7:24). The law cannot provide the answer; Jesus Christ alone provides the answer. Therefore, it is the answer of faith.

In recent exegesis, a majority of scholars read Rom 7:7–25 as written from the standpoint of one who believes in Christ, referring to Adam, the prototypical human being. With this interpretation, Rom 7:7–25 cannot be used as a proof text for the idea of *simul justus et peccator*. Nevertheless, Paul suggests that the struggle between the flesh and the spirit continues to be a danger for the believer (Gal 5:16–26). Hence, one can ask whether Romans 7 contains only a story about the past of everyone who believes. Does it not also contain a hint about a present danger of falling back under the power of sin and death because of the weakness of the flesh? In any case, "Thanks be to God through Jesus Christ our Lord!" is an important prayer for all believers who consider their past, their present, and their future.

f. Paul's criticism of boasting

Criticizing those who want to base justification on "works of the law" is linked with criticism of their boasting. Even in the letters that do not explicitly develop a theology of justification, Paul offers a critique of false boasting (1 Cor 1:29; 3:21) and speaks about a faith-inspired confidence that Christians can and should boast "in the Lord" (1 Cor 1:31; 2 Cor 10:17; 12:9).

In Rom 2:23–28, Paul criticizes boasting on the basis of the law that is countered by transgressions of the law. Using Abraham as an example, Paul says that "works of the law" may provide a basis for respect from other people but not for esteem before God (Rom 4:2). In Philippians 3, Paul criticizes those who base their boasting on belonging to the Jewish people without believing in Jesus Christ. At no time does Paul criticize faithful obedience to the commandments as such as an expression of or basis for boasting. In Rom 3:27–31, however, Paul explains that boasting cannot be overcome by the "works of the law" but only through faith in Jesus Christ—because faith is the way that men and women boast in God.

g. The fulfillment of the law

In the Letters to the Galatians and to the Romans, Paul speaks explicitly of the "fulfillment" of the law. "For the whole law is summed up in a single commandment, 'You shall love your neighbor as yourself,'" (Gal 5:14; cf. Lev 19:18). "Owe no one anything, except to love one another; for the one who loves another has fulfilled the law. The commandments, 'You shall not commit adultery; You shall not murder; You shall not steal, You shall not covet,' and any other commandment, are summed up in this word, 'Love your neighbor as yourself'" (Rom 13:8–9; cf. Lev 19:18).

The message of justification does not overthrow the law; rather, the law is upheld by the message of justification (Rom 3:31). Nonetheless, the law cannot justify anyone. Various models have been developed to describe this dialectic of Pauline theology throughout the history of Protestant and Catholic theology. These different models are expressions of particular times and particular ways of thinking.

Paul lays claim to the law as a witness for justification by faith (Rom 3:21), of which Abraham in Gen 15:6 is the clearest example.

Paul views the condemning power of the law as dialectically related to the process of redemption, since there can be no forgiveness without judgment.

As in the New Testament's Jesus tradition, the commandment to love one's neighbor is considered the crucial commandment. It is the basis on which the importance and the validity of all other commandments are explained. The commandment to love is therefore the epitome of all the commandments of the law, because in the love of neighbor the love of God, manifested in Jesus Christ, is realized.

The fulfillment of the law is a qualitative concept (cf. Matt 5:17). It points to what is eschatologically new in the Christ event. Jesus is the "yes" to all God's promises (2 Cor 1:20). He "has become a servant of the circumcised on behalf of the truth of God in order that he might confirm the promises given to the patriarchs" (Rom 15:8). The fulfillment of the law, therefore, does not occur by means of the works of the law but by means of faith in Jesus Christ, which justifies.

Justification by faith in Paul

Paul excludes justification on the basis of the works of the law. He grounds it in faith in Jesus Christ. The understanding of Paul's notion of faith explains the connection.

Faith in Jesus Christ makes concrete the faith in the one God "who gives life to the dead" (Rom 4:17). "Faith in God" is faith in the one who raised Jesus "from the dead" (1 Thess 1:10). For Paul, standing within the broad tradition of early Christianity, Jesus Christ has always been the Son of God who became human and, raised from the dead, has been exalted to God's right hand (Phil 2:6–11). In the context of justification theology, Paul writes, "if you confess with your lips that Jesus is Lord and believe in your heart that God raised him from the dead, you will be saved. For one believes with the heart and so is justified, and one confesses with the mouth and so is saved" (Rom 10:9–10).

a. Paul's understanding of faith

Because of Paul, "faith" is a key word in Christian theology. In Paul, and in other New Testament writings, faith is mentioned when there is a positive response to the missionary proclamation of the gospel and when the faithful describe the foundation of their new life.

For Paul, faith is basically a fundamental trust in God that shapes the totality of a person's life. Paul illustrates this in the Letter to the Romans using the example of Abraham:

> He did not weaken in faith when he considered his own body, which was already as good as dead (for he was about a hundred years old), or when he considered the barrenness of Sarah's womb. No distrust made him waver concerning the promise of God, but he grew strong in his faith as he gave glory to God, being fully convinced that God was able to do what he had promised. Therefore his faith "was reckoned to him as righteousness." (Rom 4:19–22)

Justifying faith is not only a faith that trusts; it is also a faith that confesses. It proclaims in what or in whom it places its trust. The first location of the confession of faith is baptism. Faith is expressed in simple confessional statements, such as, "we have come to believe in Christ Jesus" (Gal 2:16), "God is one" (Rom 3:30), "Jesus is Lord" (1 Cor 12:3; cf. Phil 3:8).

The confession of faith is proclaimed both in the first person singular (Gal 2:20) and in the first person plural (Rom 4:24; 6:8).

"I believe" expresses the existential dimension of conversion, the freedom and responsibility of faith.

"We believe" expresses the ecclesial dimension of the confession of faith, membership in the community of the faithful.

The two belong together and mutually support each other.

Justifying faith is likewise a recognition. In the Letter to the Philippians, Paul says, "I want to know Christ and the power of his resurrection and the sharing of his sufferings by becoming like him in his death, if somehow I may attain the resurrection from the dead" (Phil 3:10–11). The knowledge of faith transcends all human understanding (cf. Phil 4:7). This knowledge is a gift of the Spirit. It is authentic knowledge because it perceives the reality of the eschatological salvation which God has created in his grace.

Some recent exegetical studies have proposed that the *Christou* in the Greek phrase *pistis Christou* should be understood as a subjective genitive (the faith of Jesus Christ) rather than as an objective genitive (faith in Jesus Christ), especially when the phrase occurs in Rom 3:22; Gal 2:16; and Phil 3:9. According to this interpretation, the absolute occurrence of *pistis*, that is, the use of *pistis* without further qualification—for example, in Rom 1:7 and 3:28—should be understood as a reference to Jesus Christ's own faith and fidelity. According to that interpretation, Jesus Christ's faith is the basis for justification. Indeed, Christ's obedience to God, which Paul mentions in Rom 5:12–21 and Phil 2:6–11, is essential for Christ's salvific action. If *pistis Christou* is to be taken as a subjective genitive, then Christ's faith would be parallel to Christ's obedience, an important motif in Paul's theology. There would also be a Spirit-effected conformity between Christ, who lives to God (Rom 6:10), and Christians, who are alive "to God in Christ Jesus" (Rom 6:11). If *pistis Christou* is to be interpreted as a subjective genitive, there would also be conformity between the faith of Christ and the faith of believers who are justified. Yet it is undeniable that the basic formulations of Paul's theology of justification specify the believers' faith: "We have come to believe in Christ Jesus" (Gal 2:16). It is doubtful that the interpretation of *pistis Christou* as a subjective genitive conforms to the original meaning of the expression in Paul's letters. The christological dimension of the believers' faith is essential in Paul, and the context shows that *pistis Christou* expresses the belief of all who have become hearers of the Word (Rom 10:8–13).

b. The witness of Scripture

The scriptural foundation that Paul cites in his theology of justification does not bear on the exclusion of works of the law because that plays no role in the Old Testament reference texts; the scriptural basis of Paul's justification theology pertains only to the fundamental salvific significance of faith.

In his theology of justification, Paul explains Gen 15:6 with reference to the faith of Abraham, which is based neither on circumcision (Genesis 17) nor on the sacrifice or binding of Isaac (Genesis 22) but rather on God's promise (Genesis 12; 15): Abraham's faith is trust in God as the one who conquers the power of death and thus fulfills his promise (Romans 4). Abraham's faith is exemplary.

Other explicit scriptural proofs for the justification of those who believe are not interpreted by Paul; they are merely cited. Paul, who is convinced of the unity of Scripture, assumes that in these texts faith is to be understood in the same way that it is in Gen 15:6.

c. Faith and love

Justifying faith is intrinsically connected with love. Paul states this in a particularly succinct fashion in Gal 5:6: "For in Christ Jesus neither circumcision nor uncircumcision counts for anything; the only thing that counts is faith working through love." As is evident in the following verses, Paul means the love of one's neighbor that fulfills the law (Gal 5:14).

Paul's understanding of the relationship between faith and love is different from that of the scholastic formula "faith formed by love" (*fides caritate formata*), in which *caritas* is understood as love for God and *fides* as a reasoned confession of faith. With this understanding, the idea that love is the reality that gives faith its form makes sense. Paul's thinking, however, begins with faith. Faith develops an ability to shape the life of a Christian in freedom through love. Love of neighbor is, in turn, the energy of faith insofar as it shapes life based on a relationship with God.

From the outset, justifying faith is, for Paul, faith that is effective in love. This is clear in the Letter to the Galatians, where the first explanation of the thesis of justification (Gal 2:15–21) deals with the justified believers' way of life, determined by the love of Jesus Christ.

In the Letter to the Romans, this connection is evident in the explanations of reconciliation in chapter 5 and of baptism in chapter 6. Paul first points to the connection between God's love of his enemies and the obedience of Jesus Christ, which overcomes Adam's sin. Therefore, the apostle calls all the faithful to a life of righteousness. Against this horizon he interprets baptism as participation in the death and resurrection of Jesus and thus as participation in the ministry of righteousness accomplished by Jesus Christ himself.

The connection between faith and love clarifies why the hortatory sections of both the Letters to the Galatians and to the Romans are not appendices but essential components of Paul's theology of justification.

d. Faith in Jesus Christ as the basis for justification

For Paul, the fact that faith in Jesus Christ justifies results from the intrinsic link between the God's grace and faith. Faith turns men and women into people who affirm God with their whole heart as the father of Jesus Christ and therefore as their own "Abba, Father" (Gal 4:6; Rom 8:15).

For its part, justifying faith is not a "work of the law," even though the law testifies to the justifying power of faith. Justifying faith is entirely an act of the grace of God as well as and because of grace, a free act of the human being.

"Works of the law" are not a part of faith, neither as an addition to faith nor as an integral part of faith. "Works of the law" imply salvific faith in the law. Thereby they misunderstand the God-given meaning of the law and prevent its fulfillment. Fulfillment of the law depends on faith, effective through love.

The theology of justification in the tradition of Paul

Historical-critical exegesis differentiates between letters that were certainly written by Paul and texts written with reference to Paul and under his name. Accordingly, a major part of critical research ascribes the Epistle to the Ephesians and the Pastoral Epistles not to the apostle himself but to the New Testament's Pauline tradition. The early church attributed these letters to a later phase of Paul's work. Historical-critical exegesis places them in the late New Testament period. Canonical exegesis reveals the extent to which they have been presented as Pauline letters and have been received as such.

Neither the Epistle to the Ephesians (Eph 2:8–9) nor the Pastoral Epistles (1 Tim 1:8–9; Titus 3:5) discuss the works of the law, but, as in Rom 4:2–5; 9:12, 32; 11:6, "works" are mentioned. This is to be explained by a new challenge that had arisen. Paul had to defend the salvific sufficiency of faith in Christ against a Jewish Christian position that no one could be saved without circumcision and obedience to the law. In the Deutero-Pauline texts, that matter is no longer discussed; it is a given. Other issues arose, however, especially issues pertaining to ethics resulting from justification and the value of ethics.

a. The Epistle to the Ephesians

The church is the major theme of the Epistle to the Ephesians. Gentile Christians experience the greatness of grace insofar as they, who were "at that time without Christ, being aliens from the commonwealth of Israel, and strangers to the covenants of promise, having no hope and without God in the world" (Eph 2:12), have received full citizenship rights in the *ekklēsia* (Eph 2:19–20) according to God's eternal salvific will (Eph 1:3–14). This has occurred because Jesus, through his death and resurrection, has razed the wall that the law had erected in ordinances that distinguished Jew from Gentile (Eph 2:14–17).

Gentile Christians are to be shown that their salvation is pure grace and not due to their own merit. This is the reason why there is a reference to Paul's message of justification in Eph 2:8–9, "For by grace you have been saved through faith, and this is not your own doing; it is the gift of God—not the result of works, so that no one may boast." The works that are at issue in Ephesians are works done not because salvific significance is attributed to the law but because humans wish to boast about their own ethical and religious achievements before God. In Ephesians, as in the Letters to the Galatians and the Romans, it is faith alone that, in the unity of confession and trust, relies totally on the grace of God (Eph 2:4–7). Therefore, it is faith that saves.

b. The Pastoral Epistles

The Pastoral Epistles, 1–2 Timothy and Titus, present Paul's theology of justification in order to counter the expectation that a person can be justified or saved through works (2 Tim 1:8–9; Titus 3:5). These texts are particularly concerned with the rejection of a so-called gnosis (1 Tim 6:20). Because this "gnosis" presents a dualism that despises the physical and ascribes little value to creation, it teaches that sexual intercourse as well as certain foods and drink are impure (1 Tim 4:3–5). In response, the Pastoral Epistles argue that God has done everything for the salvation of humankind through Jesus Christ, not because of any contempt for the world but because of God's love for the world.

This new situation is connected to considerable shifts in the understanding of leading theological concepts.

In the Letters to the Galatians and the Romans, Paul understands law (*nomos*) as the covenant document of Israel and as God's way of making sin visible. In the Pastoral Epistles, *nomos* is the moral law understood from the standpoint of its being a commandment. Hence, 1 Tim 1:8–11 states that the just have no need for the law. In Galatians and Romans, however, on the one hand, trusting in salvation by means of the law is negated in principle while, on the other, the fulfillment of the law in love is propagated.

In the Letters to the Romans, the Galatians, and the Philippians, faith is the antithesis of works of the law. With the exception of 2 Tim 3:15, the Pastoral Epistles see faith not as the human being's total response to God's act of salvation but rather as essentially an assent to "sound doctrine" (1 Tim 1:10). This kind of faith is a requirement, a *conditio sine qua non*, of salvation (2 Tim 3:15), but it defines the totality of what it means to be Christian only in connection with other attitudes, especially love (*agapē*) (1 Tim 1:5, 14; 2:15; 4:12; 6:11; 2 Tim 1:13; 2:22; 3:10).

The justification of the ungodly, among whom Paul is cited as the supreme example (1 Tim 1:15), forms part of the theology of the Pastoral Epistles. This justification demonstrates the manifestation (*epiphaneia*) of "the goodness and loving kindness of our God" in the person of Jesus Christ (Titus 3:4). God's grace trains those who in faith know God's plan of salvation to lead a life in righteousness (Titus 2:12). These two affirmations of a theology of justification are in conformity with the notion of justification insofar as they reject a gnostic ethicization of soteriology and understand the righteousness necessary for salvation not as personal merit but as pure grace.

Paul in Acts: The theology of promise and salvation history

In the Lukan narrative of Acts, Paul proclaims justification by faith. In Acts, while in the synagogue of Antioch in Pisidia, Paul says, "Let it be known to you therefore, my brothers, that through this man forgiveness of sins is proclaimed to you; by this Jesus everyone who believes is set free from all those sins from which you could not be freed by the law of Moses" (Acts 13:38–39).

According to Acts, Paul and Peter agree almost word for word on the theology of justification. Looking back on his mission experiences in Caesarea (Acts 10), Peter says of God that, "in cleansing their hearts by faith he has made no distinction between them and us. Now therefore why are you putting God to the test by placing on the neck of the disciples a yoke that neither our ancestors nor we have been able to bear? On the contrary, we believe that we will be saved through the grace of the Lord Jesus, just as they will" (Acts 15:9–10).

Emphasizing the agreement between Paul and Peter, Luke pursues an ecumenical concern. Regardless of the conflicts that have taken place, Paul and Peter fundamentally agree on the theology of justification. One can, of course, distinguish the theology of justification in the speeches narrated by Luke from what Paul says in the Letters to the Galatians, the Romans, and the Philippians. But one can also discover substantial agreement. This contributes to the substance of the New Testament's witness on justification, which comes to fruition in ecumenical theology.

3. The Gospel of Jesus Christ and the Theology of Justification

While the letters of Paul are the oldest written documents in the New Testament, people often ask: What is the relationship between the gospel Paul proclaims and the gospel of Jesus Christ to which the four Gospels, especially in the earliest traditions, testify? This leads us to the next question: What do we understand by gospel of Jesus Christ?

The gospel and its different witnesses

The Gospel of Mark, the first of the four Gospels in the New Testament, begins with the line: "The beginning of the good news of Jesus Christ, the Son of God."

Using this heading Mark describes the gospel of Jesus Christ as

- The good news he preached to the people in Galilee and Judea
- The good news he brought through his healing and liberating ministry to the sick and to those who were possessed by demons, and

- The good news he lived in his death on the cross, which by his resurrection was revealed as the deepest expression of the service of his whole life, giving it as "a ransom for many."

Therefore, when examining the relationship between the gospel of Jesus Christ and the theology of justification, we will not limit ourselves to the preaching and teaching of the so-called "historical" Jesus, but will look at the understanding of the gospel in the early Jesus tradition.

There seems, however, to be a basic difference between the gospel as it is unfolded in the Jesus tradition and the gospel as it is explained by Paul.

While at the center of Paul's theology we find the statement that the righteousness of God is revealed in the gospel (Rom 1:17), at the center of the gospel of Jesus stands the proclamation that "the kingdom of God is near" (Mark 1:15; cf. Matt 4:17).

But both concepts have their roots in the eschatological expectations of Jewish apocalyptic circles, and both can be traced back to the message of Psalms 93–99 and of Second and Third Isaiah: God will reveal his righteousness and set up his reign in the near future.

John the Baptist radicalized these expectations. For him the coming of the kingdom was imminent and, with it, the final judgment that will not spare the people of God.

Jesus shared John's expectations. Nonetheless, while not denying the aspect of judgment, he put greater emphasis on the assurance that the coming of God's kingdom brings healing and liberation for those who need God's presence most.

The good news in the proclamation of the kingdom of God

This emphasis is expressed in many aspects of Jesus' preaching.

It is heard in the first Beatitude: "Blessed are you who are poor, for yours is the kingdom of God" (Luke 6:20). God's kingdom belongs to those who have nothing else to rely on and who stand with empty hands before God. When Jesus blessed the little children, we hear the same message, "for it is to such as these that the kingdom of God belongs" (Mark 10:14). Those who are unable to help themselves are the "shareholders" of the kingdom.

Wherever the Jesus tradition speaks about preaching the good news, it means good news for the poor. The background of this expression is Isa 61:1: "The Spirit of the Lord is on me, because the Lord has anointed me to preach good news to the poor" (NIV). Luke tells us that Jesus used this Scripture passage in his first sermon in Nazareth (Luke 4:18–19). Also, Jesus' answer to John the Baptist emphasizes the fact that in Jesus' preaching and healing "the poor have good news brought to them" (Matt 11:5; Luke 7:22).

Another aspect of the gospel of Jesus was his special inclination toward those who were called sinners in the society of his day. Obviously, while this was more of a sociological than a theological category, both are inextricably intertwined. Jesus approaches especially those whom society regarded as having been alienated from God and tells them that God calls precisely them into God's kingdom: "Those who are well have no need of a physician, but those who are sick; I have come to call not the righteous but sinners" (Mark 2:17). In Luke 19:10, Jesus' whole mission is summarized as follows: "For the Son of Man came to seek out and to save the lost." Two other stories, Luke 7:36–50 and John 7:53–8:11, although not a part of the original gospel, graphically illustrate the way in which Jesus dealt with such people.

The unconditional way in which Jesus accepted people into his fellowship was offensive to many people in his day, who deplored that "this fellow welcomes sinners and eats with them" (Luke 15:2). Jesus responded to them with some of his most impressive parables, especially the one of the father and the two alienated sons (Luke 15:11–36), which conveys the message of the theology of justification in the shape of a story. Both sides are represented in the story: those who are called sinners and those who call themselves righteous. Jesus does not simply say that all are sinners. Rather, all human beings can live in fellowship with God only if they follow God's gracious invitation and rejoice with him about every person who follows his invitation.

It is no coincidence that the only story in which Jesus uses the language of justification deals with a similar situation. It is the story of the Pharisee and the tax collector praying in the temple (Luke 18:9–14). Jesus' reaction to the tax collector's prayer is, "...I tell you, this man went down to his home justified rather than the other" (Luke 18:14). The story has a double message. On the one hand, it affirms those who look for mercy from God. God justifies sinners who entrust their lives to him. On the other, it warns those "who trusted in themselves that they are righteous and regard others in contempt" (Luke 18:9). The Pharisee is being criticized not for what he does but, rather, for his conviction that he can attain his position with God by comparing himself to others.

By calling the sinners to repentance and blessing the poor, Jesus preaches the essence of the message of justification.

The good news through the healing ministry of Jesus

The healing ministry was an integral part of Jesus' mission. Jesus regarded his power to deliver people from destructive demonic captivity as an important expression of the presence of the coming kingdom of God. Responding to those who criticized him for casting "out demons by Beelzebul, the ruler of the demons" (Luke 11:15), Jesus said, "if it is by the finger of God that I cast out the demons, then the kingdom of God has come to you" (Luke 11:20). In Jesus' liberating acts, the saving reign of God touches the painful reality of human life.

Jesus' answer to John the Baptist (Matt 11:4–5; Luke 7:21–22) clearly shows that Jesus' healing ministry is part of his proclamation of the gospel: "Go and tell John what you hear and see: the blind receive their sight, the lame walk, the lepers are cleansed, the deaf hear, the dead are raised, and the poor have good news brought to them." That "the poor have good news brought to them" is not an action that adds something to Jesus' healing ministry; rather, it is the summary of all that Jesus does. To heal the sick and to deliver those possessed by evil spirits are part of the good news he brings to the poor.

In the so-called *Messianic Apocalypse* from Cave 4 of Qumran (4Q521, frag. 2, col. 2), we find a similar combination of Isa 35:4–7; 61:1–2; and Ps 146:7–8: "In his mercy he will jud[ge] and from no-one shall the fruit [of] good [deeds] be delayed, and the Lord will perform marvelous acts such as have not existed, just as he has sa[id], for he will heal the badly wounded and will make the dead live, he will proclaim good news to the meek, give lavishly [to the need]y, lead the exiled and enrich the hungry." Although the first line of the text refers to God's anointed one, his Messiah, to whom heavens and earth will listen, the main emphasis is on God's own action. God will fulfill his promises and realize the hope of those who wait for him.

In light of this tradition, the full meaning of Jesus' answer to John the Baptist appears: Jesus' healing activity characterizes him as God's representative who links the coming reign of God with the suffering of the people. In healing the sick and proclaiming the good news to the poor, Jesus embodies God's eschatological righteousness, that is, God's faithfulness and mercy for those who need him most.

This corresponds to another very important aspect of Jesus' healing ministry: he helps unconditionally without posing such questions as, What have you (or your parents) done that this happened to you? Even when Jesus tells a lame man "your sins are forgiven" before healing him from his paralysis (Mark 2:1–12), this does not mean that he could only be healed after his sins had been taken away. Jesus' healing and forgiving are expressions of the unconditional "yes" God speaks in Jesus Christ to human beings.

This is highlighted by the role faith plays in Jesus' ministry. Jesus does not ask those who seek healing, and even less those possessed by demons, whether they believe in him. What he expects is that they are open to his powers of healing. The lack of such openness hinders him from performing his mighty acts in his home-town, Nazareth (Mark 6:5–6). The cry of the possessed boy's father, "I believe; help my unbelief!"(Mark 9:24) is enough to open the door for Jesus' liberating action. When the early Jesus tradition speaks about the faith of those who approach Jesus for help, it does not mention a special belief in Jesus as the Messiah. It is the persistence of the people, their "hope against hope," that qualifies their attitude toward Jesus as faith (cf. Mark 5:34). Often it is the faith not of those who need help but of those who care for them (Mark 2:5; 9:24; Matt 8:10; 15:28).

Frequently it is only after the healing has taken place that Jesus says, "Your faith has made you well" (Mark 5:34; 10:52; Luke 17:19; 8:48; Matt 9:22). This phrase could also be translated as "Your faith has saved you" (Luke 7:50; 18:42). Obviously there is a deeper dimension to Jesus' healing ministry: Here people meet the saving power of God's kingdom, which makes a human being whole in the communion with God.

Jesus addresses God's unconditional "yes" to those who suffer from alienation and are dominated by the powers of evil. They accept this "yes" and respond to it through faith. The command "Do not fear, only believe!"(Mark 5:36; Luke 8:50) in the Jesus tradition is equivalent to the *sola fide* of the message of justification in the teaching of Paul.

The good news and Jesus' death and resurrection

We are guided in the same direction when we try to understand the story of Jesus' suffering and resurrection as the deepest and most profound manifestation of the gospel. Mark's greatest achievement in writing the history of Jesus' public life as the gospel of Jesus Christ was certainly his decision to combine the traditions about Jesus' miraculous activities in Galilee with the narrative of his passion in Jerusalem and the message of his resurrection. All canonical Gospels followed Mark's basic pattern. The background of his decision was obviously the old catechetical formula that is quoted by Paul in 1 Cor 15:3–5, which describes the content of the gospel by listing the basic facts of Jesus' death and resurrection and their soteriological implication. This is the gospel and these are the events about which Paul says that in them "the righteousness of God is revealed through faith for faith" (Rom 1:17; cf. 3:21).

The oldest gospel tradition, however, was rather reluctant to interpret the meaning of Jesus' passion in theological terms. Historically, we cannot be sure how Jesus himself understood his own death. Nonetheless, already in two very early traditions, which are used by Mark and serve as key signals for the understanding of Jesus' suffering in his gospel, we find a very clear interpretation of the soteriological significance of Jesus' death and resurrection.

The first is found in Mark 10:45: "For the Son of Man came not to be served but to serve, and to give his life a ransom for many." This is a wonderful summary of Jesus' life and death under the overall theme of service as the expression of his complete pro-existence. The key word "ransom" alludes to the whole cluster of redeem—redeemer—redemption passages in the Old Testament (i.e., Isa 43:1–4) and interprets Jesus' death as the total commitment and sacrifice of his life for the sake of the liberation of human beings from their captivity under sin and death. "For many" is an allusion to Isa 53:12, where "many" is clearly not meant as a restriction of "all," but the Greek rendering of a Hebrew expression of total inclusivity.

The second statement is found in the words through which Jesus interprets the meaning of bread and cup in the last supper (Mark 14:22–24), the oldest version of which with regard to the bread is very simple: "Take; this is my body." As the bread is broken and shared at the table, so the life of Jesus will be broken and shared by those who belong to him. With regard to the cup the statement is more detailed: "This is my blood of the covenant, which is poured out for many." The Old Testament background of these words is found in Exodus 24. Just as the blood Moses sprinkled against the sides of the altar and on the people of Israel marked the new communion within the covenant God had made on Mount Sinai, so the "blood" of Jesus, his life poured out for many, constitutes the new covenant between God and humanity. Again, "many" is an allusion to Isa 53:12 and indicates the inclusive meaning of Jesus' death.

These two statements suggest how the following narrative of Jesus' suffering and resurrection should be understood. It is the story of God's "yes" to human beings, a "yes" that includes God's participation in human suffering and death, but also a "yes" that overcomes sin and death because it is the Son of God, the human representative of God's kingdom, with his irrevocable affirmation of life, who takes them upon himself. In short, Jesus' way to the cross and his resurrection are the deepest expression of God's unconditional grace.

The unity of the gospel

To sum up, the gospel of Jesus Christ, in which Jesus himself announces and lives out the coming of the kingdom of God, as well as the gospel of Jesus Christ as it is expounded in St. Paul's theology of justification are both expressions of God's eschatological "yes" to human beings. They unfold this message in a different language, but they agree that this "yes" is God's unconditional call to all who are open to sharing in his healing, liberating, and reconciling communion.

4. The Kingdom of Heaven and God's Righteousness in the Gospel of Matthew

The Gospel of Matthew can be defined as the Gospel of the kingdom of heaven that Jesus inaugurates and which will be fulfilled at the end of times. Jesus' preaching, teaching, and healing all work toward this purpose (Matt 4:21; 9:35), and the results attest that this kingdom has already arrived (Matt 12:28). A necessary decision thus follows: the beneficiaries are called to convert or to embrace the requirements of the kingdom. This kingdom, which has already started and will be perfected in the future, is not to be sought in a precise geographical space. Rather, it is a rereading of the *dikaiosynē*, a completely new understanding of justice, as the Matthean Jesus described it for the disciples or the potential recipients of the kingdom of heaven.

Even if this righteousness can be called "new" or "better" or "higher" justice (Matt 5:20, cf. *justice supérieure* [French], *bessere Gerechtigkeit* [German]), it does not negate the Jewish tradition. It is a new interpretation and takes the law beyond the way it was practiced according to the Jewish tradition. The context of the emergence of this *dikaiosynē* in the narration of Matthew will enable us better to understand the tension between an erroneous understanding of Jesus' mission, the justice of the scribes and Pharisees, and the new or higher justice. "Scribes and Pharisees" appear as literary figures of the Matthean story, not as historically reconstructed Jewish groups.

The kingdom (*basileia*) in the Gospel of Matthew

The word *basileia,* meaning "kingdom," is used fifty-four times in connection with different phrases in the Gospel of Matthew. Two of them, *basileia tou theou* (kingdom of God) and *basileia tōn ouranōn* (kingdom of heaven) are used by Matthew to signify the same reality.

Basileia is a central theological concept in the Gospel of Matthew, as in the whole Synoptic tradition. It is the motto of Jesus' proclamation. When Matthew typically designates Jesus' message as "the good news of the kingdom" (*euaggelion tēs basileias*) (Matt 4:23; 9:35; 24:14; cf. 13:19), it is because for him the church's message consists of nothing other than what Jesus has taught (cf. 28:20). The imminence of the kingdom is the content of the message of John the Baptist (Matt 3:2), Jesus (Matt 4:17), and the church (Matt 10:7). This is explicitly identified in many parables that refer to the kingdom of heaven (ch. 13). Matthew's point is that the kingdom has already arrived but is not yet complete. The coming of the kingdom of God is progressive, unfolding toward its future consummation. When Jesus uses the verb "to draw near" rather than a verb that suggests a completed action such as "has come" he probably does so intentionally. The purpose is to imply the incipient nature of the presence of the kingdom of God. Jesus can speak of the kingdom as both a present and a future reality.

Furthermore, *basileia* can mean the reality of salvation which the righteous will "inherit" (Matt 25:34) when the Son of Man accepts and justifies them at the last judgment. The use of *eiserchesthai* ("enter") in connection with *basileia* indicates that *basileia* not only carries the functional notion of sovereignty but also describes an area where the righteous will experience complete communion with God in peace and freedom. Altogether, *basileia* can represent salvation that is realized through miracles, resurrection, and the authority of the Son of God (Matt 28:18). In fact, all these representations of the kingdom are to be reached through one means, namely, the practice of *dikaiosynē*.

The *basileia* and eschatological judgment

Basileia refers to several realities. Entry into the *basileia* is promised to those who achieve a better righteousness (Matt 5:20), to the one who does the will of the Father (Matt 7:21), and to the one who repents and becomes humble like a child (Matt 18:3). In some cases, the kingdom is also coupled with the concept of a final judgment, which is highlighted in many parables (cf. Matt 13:41–43, 49–50; 18:34–35; 20:16; 22:11–14; 25:12–13, 29–30). Then the "end of the age" (Matt 28:20) will come. The king will separate the righteous from the unrighteous (Matt 7:21–23), the sheep from the goats (Matt 25:31–46), the wheat from the tares (Matt 13:37–43). Those who have not done the Father's will (7:21), who have not believed in Christ (18:6), will merit eternal punishment (13:42; 25:46), but the righteous will enter into eternal life (13:43; 25:34, 46).

In Matthew, righteousness is very much connected with the notion of judgment and forgiveness. The disciples are encouraged to expect God's gracious forgiveness, but they are also told that those who do not forgive will not be forgiven. The parable of the unjust servant illustrates the immensity of God's forgiveness. But Matthew's paraenetic interests led him to add a warning, namely, that a forgiving master punishes the servant who does not forgive (Matt 18:23–35). Also, the Lord's Prayer indicates that the forgiveness of others is a condition for receiving the blessing of forgiveness associated with the coming of the kingdom (Matt 6:12, 15).

The theology of God's righteousness according to Matthew

Understanding the concept of righteousness in the Gospel of Matthew requires elucidating the social and religious context in which the author defines it. Obviously, the Gospel of Matthew faces a historical challenge: the author and his community are in the middle of a debate about the meaning of the law for those who believe in Christ. According to Matthew, the understanding of righteousness is marked by different conceptions relating to the law, namely, either to abolish it completely or to observe all its precepts (Matt 5:17). Jesus opposes the position of a group of Christian believers and their understanding of his coming and his mission. They thought that Jesus had come in order to remove or declare invalid "the law and the prophets" (Matt 7:12). But the "law and the prophets" are to be regarded as expressing God's will, a concept broader than precept or command.

Nevertheless, the understanding of righteousness in the Gospel of Matthew cannot be restricted to this conflict about the law. In fact, the first occurrence of the word *righteousness* refers to the coming of Jesus to John the Baptist (Matt 3:15). Jesus' baptism by John is meant "to fulfill all righteousness." Moreover, already the coming of John the Baptist as a parallel to the coming of Jesus can be seen as a coming "in the way of righteousness" (Matt 21:32). Therefore, Matthew understands Jesus' mission as an expression of the will of God as described in the law and by the prophets.

Jesus thus establishes righteousness as God's eschatological will and the law as the standard against which Christian ethics are to be measured. According to Matt 5:17–20, the significance of the law within the Christian community derives from Jesus' authoritative decree, emphasized by the repeated use of the personal pronoun "I." The transgressor of the law "will be called least in the kingdom of heaven." God will honor the one who respected the least requirements of the law (Matt 5:19). Obedience to the whole law is what counts in the kingdom of heaven, which only those will enter who, like children, do not bargain for a reward and whose righteousness is focused on God's entire will (Matt 18:1–5; 5:20).

Jesus affirms two things in Matt 5:17–19: Christians should not believe that his presence means the easing or the abrogation of the precepts of the law but, on the contrary, from now on Christians must be those who more than anyone else do not have the right to scorn the least requirement.

In Matt 5:20, *dikaiosynē* is put forward as the criterion of salvation. It is a righteousness that is not to be considered apart from the Torah. The antitheses of the Sermon on the Mount (Matt 5:21–48) are an explanation of what the Matthean Jesus calls righteousness and should lead the disciples to perfection "as your heavenly Father is perfect" (Matt 5:48). Jesus establishes the new understanding of the law, defined in opposition to the concept of the "scribes and Pharisees." *Dikaiosynē* indicates behavior in conformity with God's will.

Righteousness—gift and call

There is a difference between the Matthean understanding of the Torah and that of the "scribes and the Pharisees." "You have heard that it was said to those of ancient times..., But I say to you that..." (Matt 5:21–22; cf. 5:27, 31, 33, 38, 43). Jesus thereby quotes the traditional understanding of righteousness, before calling it into question. The transition in question here is introduced by the Greek coordinating conjunction *de*, which can be understood either as a contrast or as a means of stressing the semantics. Jesus' own understanding of the will of God is placed in opposition to the traditional understanding of the Torah. Repetition highlights the importance of this semantic opposition (5:21, 22, 27, 28, 31, 32, 33, 34, 38, 39, 43, 44). Jesus' declaration not only affirms that which was transmitted by the tradition, but exceeds it by reinforcing it.

The traditional reading of the law stops at the level of such visible acts as committing murder (Matt 5:21), committing adultery (Matt 5:27), repudiating one's wife (Matt 5:33), and perjuring oneself (Matt 5:33). But the Matthean Jesus conceives of justice beyond what can be observed: those who permit themselves to become angry have already committed a murder; the one who only looks at a woman to covet her has already committed adultery. This position is justified by the declaration in Matt 6:1: "Beware of practicing your piety before others in order to be seen by them; for then you have no reward from your Father in heaven." Here Jesus reproaches the "Pharisees" for their "righteousness," since they practice their piety in order to be appreciated by others. Their acts such as almsgiving, fasting, or prayer are meant as an exhibition in the synagogues and at the crossroads (Matt 6:1–5, 16). Matthew does not call into question the law, but he gives it a more personal and complete meaning.

Justice is not limited to that which is visible; it includes what is conceived in the secrecy of the heart. Justice no longer consists merely of applying a certain set of moral rules; it now involves examining the disciple's interior, that invisible part of a person that is visible to God alone. Only God can see that place where the motives for certain acts are born, the place from which one can understand the believer. Justice emanates from this place, hidden from the human eye yet controlled by Christ, who alone can change the human value system and allow the disciple to practice the "new" justice.

The Matthean interpretation of the law is a call to perfection (Matt 5:48). Jesus wants to underline the fact that the practical application of the law alone does not suffice in the kingdom, since the practical application of the law may be merely a pretension (Matt 23:3). Practicing the law may, for instance, hide blindness and pride that lead to overestimating oneself and to contempt of others (Matt 7:1–5). In other words, Jesus is the true master of justice, and it is only through him that one can aspire to the "higher justice" that leads to the kingdom of heaven. Contrary to the justice of the "Pharisees," which is the result of a personal effort, higher justice is a gift from God. It is defined not by obedience to the precepts of the law but by total dependence on God. In Matthew's words, "strive first for the kingdom of God and his righteousness, and all these things will be given to you as well" (Matt 6:33).

This is already confirmed by the Matthean Beatitudes, where Jesus affirms that the kingdom of heaven belongs to the "poor in spirit" (Matt 5:3). According to Matt 5:6, Jesus praised "those who hunger and thirst for righteousness" for they will be satisfied. Indeed, hunger and thirst indicate a burning desire and are needs of both the heart and the body. Really hungry and thirsty persons have reached their limits. The righteousness to which the needy aspire is not only social justice, but the sovereign verdict of God, who delivers the oppressed. Being hungry and thirsty for righteousness means to desire a relationship of obedience to and confidence in God.

Righteousness as paradoxical justice

Jesus' teaching and actions embody the "new justice," which does not derogate from human laws, but falls under the logic of the command to love (Matt 22:37–40). In other words, this righteousness supersedes the law whenever it violates human dignity. It is a "paradoxical justice" insofar as Jesus has not come to call "the righteous" but sinners (cf. Matt 9:13). This exceeds the limits imposed by the law. On several occasions, Jesus is in discussion with the "scribes and the Pharisees," who criticize his attitude for not conforming to that of the righteous according to the Jewish tradition. For example, he touches lepers, who symbolize impurity (Matt 8:1–4); he cures a Gentile's servant (Matt 8:5–13); he violates the Sabbath (Matt 12:1–8); he eats with "sinners" (Matt 9:10–11; 11:19); his disciples do not comply with the rules of ablutions (Matt 15:1–9); he offers a new view of impurity (Matt 15:10–20); he converses with a foreign woman and cures her daughter (Matt 15:21–28). In the parable of the laborers in the vineyard (Matt 20:1–16), Jesus pleads with unexpected logic, for the goodness of God provides all they need and calls into question the request for adequate remuneration.

While the Pharisees regard Jesus' different dealings as being contrary to law, Matthew presents them as the "higher justice," because their aim is to meet the neighbor's need and to fulfill the practical application of the love commandment. When Jesus says that his disciples must be "perfect" (Matt 5:48), he means that they should be mature and inclusive in their regard for others. Jesus explains to his disciples that love is to be extended to every person, even to one's enemies: "But I tell you: Love your enemies and pray for those who persecute you, that you may be sons of your Father in heaven. He causes his sun to rise on the evil and the good, and sends rain on the righteous and the unrighteous" (Matt 5:44–45). Righteousness is both a gift and a task, a call that mobilizes the disciples to focus on others. It is a balanced harmony between God's gift and what is expected of us.

The kingdom of heaven and the theology of righteousness

The Gospel of Matthew can be understood as the transition from the concept of law to that of righteousness. The letter of the law gives way to justice; what is important is the aim of the law. Rather than obedience to the letter of the law, what is decisive instead is the revelation of justice that offers a new understanding of God, of oneself, and of others. The one who fails to see in the law (in the light of Christ) the promise of a new understanding of God, of oneself, and of others, cannot enter the kingdom of heaven. Matthew holds two contrasting elements in creative tension: the *law as a command*, applicable to one's place in the kingdom of heaven, and *righteousness* which is the fulfillment by Christ of the "law and the prophets." Thus the first will of God is brought to light. In his narrative and theological perspective, Matthew introduces Jesus as the promoter of the kingdom of heaven to which access is subject to practicing the "new" justice. A close relationship exists between the kingdom of heaven and justice, and entry into the kingdom is conditional on justice or righteousness, which Jesus Christ himself has brought and taught.

Righteousness according to Matthew and justification according to Paul

The Matthean concept of justice has a specific profile, especially compared to the way in which Paul makes use of the biblical tradition of justice and righteousness. When Matthew speaks of righteousness, human behavior in perfect conformity with the will of God is central. With regard to the last judgment, Matthew emphasizes the disciples' efforts to follow God's commandments and the readiness to forgive one another. The Letter of James points in a similar direction, emphasizing that faith and works belong together and that the day of judgment has to be borne in mind.

Yet Matthew's understanding of righteousness cannot be played off against the Pauline doctrine of justification. One has to keep in mind that also in Paul there is an inseparable relationship between the saving act of justification and its consequences for the life of the believers. And, when Matthew speaks of righteousness, this includes not only ethics or the last judgment. According to Matthew, Jesus himself is the first to fulfill all righteousness by his coming into the world and his way on the cross (Matt 3:15). Those who "hunger and thirst for righteousness" (Matt 5:6) are blessed. Matthew asks his disciples to follow in Jesus' footsteps by doing what is right before God.

5. The Doctrine of Justification from a Johannine Perspective

The Johannine Gospel, that is, the good news as presented in the Fourth Gospel and the three Letters of John, is relatively modest in its use of the explicit language of justification. The mission statement in John 16:7–11, which says that when the Advocate comes he will prove the world wrong about righteousness, and the threefold mention of doing righteousness in 1 John 2:28–3:10, "[e]veryone who does what is right is righteous, just as he is righteous" (1 John 3:7), are two notable exceptions in this regard. Nevertheless, much of the theology associated with the doctrine of justification appears in the Johannine Gospel, albeit in typically Johannine idiom and from a distinctively Johannine perspective.

Human sinfulness

The First Letter of John emphasizes the sinfulness of believers, maintaining, "If we say that we have no sin, we deceive ourselves....If we say that we have not sinned, we make him a liar" (1 John 1:8, 10). Acknowledging sin is a condition of forgiveness, for, "[i]f we confess our sins, he who is faithful and just will forgive us our sins and cleanse us from all unrighteousness" (1 John 1:9). While the forgiveness of sins comes from God, the just and faithful one, forgiveness of sin is mediated through Jesus Christ, who was revealed to take away sins (1 John

3:5). He is "the Lamb of God who takes away the sin of the world!" (John 1:29). On account of the name of Jesus, sins are forgiven (1 John 2:12). Sin remains with those who do not believe in Jesus (John 9:41; cf. 8:24; 12:46; 16:8–9).

The Father's initiative

The divine initiative, that is, the Father's initiative in the drama of salvation, is underscored throughout the Johannine corpus. "For God so loved the world that he gave his only Son, so that everyone who believes in him may not perish but may have eternal life. Indeed, God did not send the Son into the world to condemn the world, but in order that the world might be saved through him" (John 3:16–17; cf. 1 John 4:10) is but one passage among many that highlight the Father's initiative of sending the Son for the sake of our salvation.

Proceeding from the Father's love, the mission of the Son is an entirely gratuitous act on the Father's part. Salvation is the gift of the Father, who works through the Son. "The Father loves the Son and has placed all things in his hands" (John 3:35; cf. 13:3; 17:24). As the Father loves the Son, so the Son loves his disciples. There is a chain of love that links the love of the Father for the Son (John 10:17; 15:9; 17:26) to the Son's love for his disciples (John 13:1, 34; 15:9, 12), which enables them to love one another (cf. 1 John 4:11). The command that they love one another (John 13:34; 15:17) is Jesus' enabling gift (cf. 1 John 3:23).

Belief in the Son

To accept the Son and receive salvation is to believe in the Son, but belief is possible only to the extent that it is enabled by the Father. "No one can come to me unless drawn by the Father who sent me; and I will raise that person up on the last day," said the Johannine Jesus to his disciples (John 6:44; cf. 6:37). The ability to come to Jesus is the Father's gift (*dedomenon...ek tou patros*; John 6:65).

Belief in the Son leads to life (John 3:36). In Johannine terms, life that is concomitant with belief is eternal life (*zōē aiōnios*; see John 3:15, 16, 36; 4:14, 36; 5:24, 39; 6:27, 40, 47, 54, 68; 10:28; 12:25, 50; 17:2, 3; cf. 1 John 1:2; 2:25; 3:15; 5:11, 13, 20), Jesus' gift (John 10:28; 17:2) and the Spirit's gift (John 6:63). The Spirit himself is a gift that is bestowed upon us (John 14:16–17; 1 John 3:24; 4:13), a gift given without limitation (John 3:34; cf. 7:39a). Ultimately, eternal life is God's gift, and this life is life in God's son (1 John 5:11–12). It is the Father's will that all who see the Son and believe in him may have eternal life (John 6:40). Jesus' being lifted up on the cross was necessary so that whoever believes in him may have eternal life (John 3:15).

A chain of life

As there is a chain of love from the Father's love through the Son's love to the disciples' love for one another, so there is also a chain of life from the Father through the Son (John 5:26) to the disciples: "Just as the living Father sent me and I live because of the Father, so the one who feeds on me will live because of me" (John 6:57). The parable of the true vine (John 15:1–17) speaks of this life as a mutual indwelling between Jesus and his disciples: "I am the vine, you are the branches. Those who abide in me and I (*ho menōn en emoi kagō*) in them bear much fruit, because apart from me you can do nothing" (John 15:5; cf. 6:56; 15:4, 6). In this the Father takes the initiative since the Father is the vine grower (John 15:1). Indeed, since the Father abides in Jesus and Jesus in the Father (John 14:10–11), the mutual indwelling between Jesus and his disciples shares in the mutual indwelling between the Father and Jesus.

Life begins with being born of water and the Spirit (John 3:5), a birth that is from above (John 3:3), birth that is from the Spirit (John 3:6). Life is sustained by eating the flesh of the Son of Man and drinking his blood (John 6:50, 51, 54). This life is eternal life and culminates in one's being raised on the last day (John 6:54). Eating the flesh of the Son of Man and drinking his blood is the living bread come down from heaven, Jesus' gift (John 6:27, 51). Ultimately, this is the Father's gift, for "it is my Father who gives you the true bread from heaven" (John 6:22).

The Father's gifts

Throughout the Fourth Gospel there is an emphasis on the Father's gift mediated by the Son (cf. John 16:23). Among the words the evangelist uses very frequently to describe action is the verb "give" (*didōmi*). The verb appears eighty times in the Fourth Gospel. In most instances, this verb is used to describe what the Father has given to the Son and what the Son gives to those who believe in him, that is, the Father's gift (*dōrean tou theou*, John 4:10) mediated through the Son. The dialogue between Jesus and the Samaritan woman (John 4:7–15) highlights Jesus' life-giving gift, gushing up to eternal life.

These gifts must be seen in the light of the prologue's all-encompassing statement, "to all who received him, who believed in his name, he gave power to become children of God" (John 1:12; cf. 1 John 3:1). They cannot sin because they have been born of God (1 John 3:9). Contrary to doing what is sinful is doing what is right, and the one who does what is right is righteous (*ho poiōn tēn dikaiosynēn dikaios estin*), just as the Son of God is righteous (1 John 3:7).

By emphasizing the fact that only those who believe in Jesus Christ as the Son of God will receive eternal life (John 3:16; 11:25–26; 20:31), Johannine theology makes totally clear that to be able to do what is righteous is entirely a gift of God. Salvation is nothing other than "grace upon grace" (John 1:16).

Paul, Matthew, and John

With a terminology and a theological approach that differ from those of Paul, Johannine theology proclaims the priority of God's grace and the centrality of faith as the human response that is so important in the Pauline doctrine of justification. John emphasizes God's love as the source of the salvific event, the importance of the sending or mission of Jesus, the lifting up of Jesus on the cross, and of belief as leading to eternal life (cf. John 3:14–17). Judgment is already taking place insofar as a person believes or not (John 3:18–19); of this judgment the Spirit will convince the world (John 16:11).

Together with Paul and Matthew, the Fourth Gospel proclaims that the faith-based relationship with Jesus leads to a way of life that can be described in terms of keeping the commandments (John 14:21). Indeed, "everyone who does what is right is righteous, just as he is righteous" (1 John 3:7).

6. God's Righteousness in the Letter of James

God as the giver of good gifts

"Every generous act of giving, with every perfect gift, is from above" (Jas 1:17). This maxim is characteristic of the understanding of God in the Letter of James: In the first instance, God is the giver of good gifts (Jas 1:5, 7, 12, 17; 3:15, 17); humans receive them. Works do not "make" the person; rather, it is what a person is willing to receive from God that makes a person who they are. Accordingly, statements in the passive voice define the image of the human being in the Letter of James: The blessed man (cf. Ps 1:1) will receive the crown of life that the Lord has promised (Jas 1:12). In contrast, God is active as Creator (Jas 1:18; 3:9) and "Father" (Jas 1:17), who is immediately afterwards described by the specifically maternal trait of giving birth (Jas 1:18). God comes to help those who turn to him (Jas 4:8; 5:14–15) and hears the cries of the suffering (Jas 5:4). As judge (Jas 2:13; 4:9, 12; 5:9), God can preserve life and save or not (Jas 4:12, 15; 5:19–20). God raises up the lowly and brings down the proud (Jas 2:5; 4:6, 10).

The use of righteousness in James

In the Letter of James, there is little mention of God's righteousness and the justification of human beings. In Jas 1:20 it is said, "your anger does not produce God's righteousness." From its context this sentence conclusively inverts a statement about God's appreciation of humans' righteous deeds. Humans cannot achieve this appreciation by God; they can only receive the saving word (Jas 1:21b). Abraham and Rahab, the harlot, are cited as biblical examples that God recognizes human activity that expresses and perfects faith (Jas 2:21, 23, 24, 25).

The law in the Letter of James

In the Letter of James, the Torah belongs to God's gifts to the believers. As "a perfect law of freedom" it works like a mirror in which believers recognize their faces as creatures of God, which the believer, as a doer of the Word, not only a hearer, shall permanently preserve (Jas 1:22–25). This shows that even in the Letter of James the Torah at first is not a demand. This understanding of the law is of a piece with the addressees of the letter being called "the twelve tribes in the Dispersion" (Jas 1:1), therefore as belonging to Israel. For Israel, the Torah is the gift of God and a norm for life as a consequence of Israel's being the chosen people. Nothing in the Letter of James indicates that for the addressees of the letter—as in the Pauline communities—the Torah is regarded as a boundary marker between Jews and Gentiles. The Torah remains as an expression of God's will that is worthwhile following, in one's daily life, in regard to neighbor and God.

Faith and works according to James

In the Letter of James, as far as human salvation is concerned (Jas 1:12–25), receiving (Jas 1:12, 21) and listening (Jas 1:22–23) are mentioned rather than faith or works. From these contexts, faith cannot be misunderstood as a "justifying work." When faith and works are presented together in James, the unity of hearing and acting, of believing and living, is the topic at hand (Jas 2:14–26); the origin of faith is no longer at stake.

James 2:14–26 is to be understood as a digression from the letter's main line of argument. Nonetheless, the emphasis James places on the interrelationship between faith and works provides a hint as to his main intentions in writing the letter. This intention is guided by the exhortation to be a doer, not only a hearer, of God's salvific word (Jas 1:22). The context shows that faith must be expressed in action. Faith and works are combined in the Letter of James only when the development and shaping of the new life, which believers received as a gift from God, is at hand. Therefore, faith is expressed in works (Jas 2:18), but it is not produced by them. It is apparent from the acts, whether or not one has received the good gift of belief (cf. also Jas 3:13).

The particularity of the statements about God's righteousness and the justification of humans in the Letter of James consists also of this, that the action of the believer is certainly taken into consideration, not as the prerequisite or condition for the reception of salvation, but rather as the consequence of faith. In James, works are the expressions of faith. They bear witness to the fact that a person has received faith that is living within him or her.

Faith and works in James and justification in Paul

In comparison with Paul, the differences are remarkable. Whereas in Paul the "righteousness of God–justification of humans–faith" vocabulary refers to the inclusion of all humankind in the salvific activity of God, characterized by the Christ event, in James the same vocabulary is used to present the life and activity of human beings as the consequence of faith, which they have previously received as a gift.

The most important difference between James and Paul is the relevance of the Torah with regard to faith. This difference can be seen in the fact that the expression "works of the law" occurs only in Paul, never in James. Whereas, according to Paul, the Torah has no role in accessing the salvific power of the Christ event, in James the Torah is part of God's saving activity on behalf of his people.

In comparison with Paul, James is closer to the understanding of the law and usage of language that were widespread in early Judaism. James's understanding of righteousness is more related to Matthew's concept of justice than it is to the Pauline theology of justification. Nevertheless, the ways in which the "righteousness of God–justification–faith" vocabulary is used by the two New Testament authors should not be merged, nor are they mutually exclusive. Rather, they must be understood within their respective contexts and not be set in opposition to one another.

The Letter of James and the biblical theology of justification

To expand and deepen the biblical basis for the doctrine of justification, the Letter of James, along with other New Testament witnesses, provides a fruitful development of the apostolic Christian witness.

- Read in the canonical context of the New Testament, with the figure of James as the author of the letter, the letter appears as the voice of a relative of Jesus. The brother of the Lord as an apostolic witness to Christ provides a personal link between the activity, the way, and the fate of Jesus and his presence within his community as the Risen One.
- With the letter's exhortation about doing what is right (for example, "the harvest of righteousness," Jas 3:18) the visible side of the living faith is expressed as the inevitable consequence of the reception of "the word of truth" (Jas 1:18). The leitmotif of the letter consists of an exhortation on the unity of faith and life, word and deed.
- That such a living, visible faith is a consequence of the Christ event, not its prerequisite, results from the theologically central statements about the reception of the word (Jas 1:18). In the Letter of James, the salvific activity of God precedes and exposes human action.
- The Letter of James brings to a particular clarity the reality of the Christ event as a gift. God appears as the salvific actor; human beings as receivers of God's good gifts.
- The faith paraenesis of the Letter of James provides a constitutive component of the New Testament (and Old Testament) witness to a living faith resulting from the Christ event.

7. The New Testament and the Theology of Justification

Our exegetical analysis has shown that the theology of justification is an indispensable theological key to the gospel of Jesus Christ as it is witnessed in the entire New Testament. This does not mean that the language of justification is present on every page of the New Testament or in each one of the New Testament writings. There is a great theological richness of different narratives, confessions, metaphors, and motifs that all are able to testify to essential aspects of the way in which God acts in Jesus Christ for the salvation of God's people and all human beings. The different theological outlines within the New Testament are based on the conviction that it is God's love that realizes God's universal will of salvation through Jesus Christ in the power of the Holy Spirit. God accepts those who had been estranged from God and shapes their lives according to his will.

In Paul's main letters, the theology of justification marks the decisive criterion for the whole gospel, because it focuses most clearly on the forgiving, liberating, renewing, and communion-building power of God's revelation through the life, death, and resurrection of Jesus Christ. Paul developed his theology of justification in a situation when the freedom of the believers and the inclusive nature of his mission were in danger. Nonetheless, the basic convictions that led him to the precise formulation of this theology were constitutive for his preaching, teaching, and pastoral care during his whole ministry as far as we can see in his letters. For Paul, the theology of justification is common teaching shared by Peter and the whole community of apostles (Gal 2:15–16).

Just because it was developed in the struggle about the nature and the scope of the apostolic mission, the Pauline theology of justification is not an abstract theory about how sinners may be saved. The message of justification is the theological expression of the unconditional acceptance of all human beings by the grace of God. Its origin is missional; its goal ecumenical. It has social consequences regarding the inclusive nature of the body of Christ, and it is the basis for a new life shaped by the love of God and love of neighbor.

The notion that we are justified "apart from works of the law" had its special meaning in Paul's struggle with those who argued that circumcision is necessary in order to belong to the people of God. Paul reflects this problem in such a radical way that the theology of justification with its antithesis "justified not by the works of the law but through faith in Jesus Christ" (Gal 2:16) hits the core of human life before God. It critiques not only human boasting of religious achievements before God but also any limitation or condition for God's will to save by reference to human traditions, even when they seem to be of highest religious importance.

At the same time, the theology of justification is an expression of the gospel, which makes clear why it is faith that effects the full participation of Jews and Gentiles in the people of God, founding the hope of participation in the coming kingdom of God. Already Ephesians and the Pastoral Epistles translate this message in a new situation, while Acts narrates the history of mission in a way showing that Peter and Paul agree in the theology of justification.

In terms of theology, there is deep equivalence between Pauline theology and the basic gospel of Jesus Christ as represented by the early gospel tradition. In the Synoptic Gospels, the term "justification" appears only once, namely, in Jesus' comment on the parable of the Pharisee and the tax collector (Luke 18:9–14): "this man went down to his home justified rather than the other." But the message of justification draws the theological consequence from the gospel of Jesus Christ, that is, the good news that Jesus proclaimed and lived and which was sealed by his death and affirmed for all through his resurrection. In the way Jesus cared for the sick, liberated those possessed by evil spirits, blessed the poor, had fellowship with sinners, and gave his life as a "ransom for many" (Matt 20:28; Mark 10:45), God's love, which seeks to bring the lost children home to God's kingdom, became a reality in the midst of human suffering, sin, and death. It is this reality that Paul wants to characterize when he speaks of the "justification of the ungodly."

Among the four Gospels, Matthew especially saw the "gospel of the kingdom" as being connected with the imminent presence and the coming fulfillment of God's righteousness. God's righteousness is an undeserved gift: Those "who hunger and thirst for righteousness," will be filled with it (Matt 5:6). This is also a call. "But strive first for the kingdom of God and his righteousness" (Matt 6:33) is the imperative that follows the indicative of the Beatitudes. Somewhat different from Paul's theology of justification, yet basically from the same perspective, Matthew describes God's righteousness as the saving power and the ultimate challenge for the lives of human beings.

The Johannine tradition has a different emphasis. Concentrating on the revelation of God's love and God's glory in the life and death of Jesus, the "Son," Johannine theology proclaims in its own way the power of God's grace and the centrality of faith in the human response. "God is love" (1 John 4:8–16) is one of the basic statements about God's nature in the entire New Testament. It is verified in Jesus' affirmation in John 3:16 that "God so loved the world that he gave his only Son" for the salvation of all who believe. This comes very close to the way in which for Paul the assurance of God's love is the basis of his doctrine of justification (Rom 5:5–10; 8:31–39). Johannine theology expresses what is meant by justification in its full meaning without using the language of justification.

The Letter of James is often seen as openly contradicting the Pauline message of justification. The letter clearly offers at least a kind of contrasting model to what could be perceived as a dangerous interpretation of Paul's teaching. Closer examination, however, has shown that his model is not a contradiction to the intention of Paul's theology. For James, too, God's saving activity precedes and exposes human action. His contrasting method shows with particular clarity the reality that the Christ event is a gift. God is always seen as the one who acts for our salvation and humans as those who receive God's good gifts.

It would be interesting to investigate also other New Testament writings. We would possibly find that there are some that are very close to the intention of Paul's doctrine of justification, for example, the Gospel of Mark or First Peter, with their special emphasis on the theology of the cross. We may find others whose theology in many respects is closely related to what Paul wants to express through his theology of justification but which reveal also other emphases that seem to be foreign to this message, for example, Hebrews or the Book of Revelation. Challenging here would be not simply to add other themes to the message of justification or simply to avoid or neglect these concerns, but rather to integrate them through a process of critical hermeneutical reflection. We are convinced that in such a process the doctrine of justification would prove itself as the master and lodestar for our interpretation of the gospel as it is witnessed to in the New Testament.

VI

The Bible and the *JDDJ*—Conclusion

What insights have we gained from our study and what have we learned from the different contributions and our joint rereading of the biblical texts?

1. General Insights

We once again experienced what biblical scholars discovered already half a century ago: ecumenical exegesis is possible. While as exegetes and theologians we do not always share a common understanding of biblical notions and texts and differ in our methodological approaches, these differences very seldom coincide with the historical divisions between our denominational traditions. And even if we have the impression that some emphases in the interpretation of Scripture are typical of a Catholic or Lutheran or Methodist or Reformed approach, we are able to recognize the common ground that lies in our understanding of the biblical witness to God's saving action in the history of Israel and the life, death, and resurrection of Jesus Christ.

The broader biblical horizon has deepened our understanding of both the Old Testament witness to God's righteousness and the New Testament message of God's liberating and justifying action in Jesus Christ. We have discovered the importance of the Old Testament as it reveals the connection between God's creative and sustaining righteousness, between the way God lays the foundation for righteous relationships of human beings and the quest for righteousness among them, and especially between God's just judgment and readiness to forgive and to accept those who appeal to his righteousness and mercy. The Old Testament is not the dark background against which the light of the Pauline theology of justification shines all the brighter, but the foundation on which the whole doctrine is built.

We hope that this study may also serve as a contribution to the Christian–Jewish dialogue. It should have become clear that the theology of justification is not an anti-Jewish polemic (*Kampfeslehre*). The controversy regarding whether Gentiles have to become Jews before they can join the church and take part in communion with Christ may have produced arguments that seem to be critical of the Jewish approach to the law and the Jewish understanding of the way of salvation as Paul saw it. But this critique never goes beyond what some Old Testament prophets had to say to Israel, and never relinquishes the solidarity with God's chosen people and the deep conviction that God has not forsaken his people.

2. Exegetical Insights

The most important result of this study is the realization that there is a common biblical witness to God's saving action that precedes every human effort and overcomes all that separates God's people from God. In the Old Testament, this is exemplified by the relationship between God and the people of Israel. There are also indications that this may also hold true for the relationship between God and the nations, and between Creator and his creation in general.

There is also a common biblical witness to the fact that the goal of God's saving action is the human response to it. It is a response through which those who are rescued and liberated place their whole existence into God's hands and are enabled freely to obey God's will. To respond is not an achievement on the behalf of human beings. Rather, it fulfills what God has intended to achieve through gracious action, namely, a new and integral relationship with those God has created and called to be his people.

Although there are different "theologies of salvation" in different layers of the biblical tradition, there is a basic, common "structure" in the understanding of God's work and human reaction.

The theology of justification, especially in its elaborated Pauline version, plays a threefold role within these different theologies of salvation.

- The theology of justification is the basis for a universal theology of mission. That God is the God not only of the Jews but also of the Gentiles is a consequence of the basic confession of Israel, the Shema Yisrael; but it is the theology of justification that transforms this confession into the call to proclaim to all people the revelation of God's righteousness in the gospel of Jesus Christ.
- The theology of justification is the basis for a theology of *koinōnia* which constitutes the church as a reconciled diversity of people of different ethnic, cultural, and religious backgrounds as well as different theological and spiritual insights. This is possible because Christ and God's love, which is revealed in him, are the foundation of the church and its communion.

- The theology of justification offers the deepest insight into the human condition before God. How extreme the distance and even the enmity between human beings and God is becomes visible only in the light of God's all-encompassing and reconciling love in the death of his Son on the cross. Our incapacity as human beings to do anything to restore the broken communion with God becomes apparent only through the recognition that God has already done all that is necessary to reconcile us with him. Only God's undeserved grace enables us as human beings to be competent witnesses to this grace, servants of his righteousness, ambassadors of Christ, and coworkers for God's peace.

It is evident that there is a "surplus" in the biblical understanding of justice and righteousness above the classical conception of the doctrine of justification that dealt mainly with the question of how the individual is saved by faith through God's grace. This message—so precious to the Reformation—is neither denied nor superseded by the new and broader perspective on the biblical witness to God's righteousness and justification. But it is put within a wider context which may help us not only to understand the whole of the biblical message in a better way but also to come to terms with issues of today.

3. Conclusions Regarding the *JDDJ*

In terms of historical analysis, the different biblical concepts may appear somewhat unrelated. While some may seem to be connected with one another, others may give the impression of being contradictory. To be able to interpret their complex relationship theologically we need a hermeneutical key, a center of the whole, which shows us the interdependence of the different emphases in the various traditions. This is the critical function of the theology of justification with regard to the different biblical traditions. In its classical form, as it is developed in the *JDDJ*, it explains the soteriological core of the biblical message, which quasi-illuminates from the inside what God's gracious intention is regarding human beings and what this means for their relationship with him. That is the reason why the doctrine of justification is the "measure or touchstone for the Christian faith."[1]

Nonetheless, there is also a mutual critical function of the different traditions of salvation theology in the Bible. The center does not exhaust the whole reality. Looking at the different expressions of the revelation of God's righteousness and at various forms of experience of God's justifying and liberating grace in the biblical tradition helps to avoid any narrowing of the scope of the biblical view of God's saving action. The often-deplored individualization of the biblical message in Western theology can be overcome by taking into account the richness of the biblical witness without losing the personal depth of the message of justification by faith.

To a certain extent, the multiplicity of biblical approaches may be seen as an analogy to the different confessional understandings, although it would be too simplistic merely to identify our different theological and ecclesial traditions with different writings or traditions in the New Testament. The truth in this analogy is that we are called to listen to the spiritual and theological insights of others just as we are called to be open to the shape of the Gospel which challenges us in its diverse expressions in different strands of the biblical witness. That these different traditions are put together as the Scripture of the church shows that their diversity includes a call to unity. Some areas of our disagreements may mirror differences in the biblical witnesses, but it is precisely these that urge us to look for a biblically differentiated consensus that may be the base of a differentiated consensus between our traditions. The *JDDJ* is a first step in this direction. Our biblical study has shown that the most problematic topics for a common understanding of the doctrine of justification, as mentioned in chapter 4 of the *JDDJ* (*JDDJ,* 19–39), can be solved by way of a differentiated consensus. Of course, the discussion in the sixteenth century differed in many aspects from the biblical settings; this became obvious during our study, too. But to consider the broader biblical basis of the doctrine of justification helps us to put into perspective the traditional controversies and to deepen the consensus.

In view of the ongoing discussion, our joint efforts to understand the biblical witness may also challenge some key elements of our own traditions and question their scriptural basis, which we have taken for granted. It is true that the Jesus tradition speaks about "reward"; but the theology of justification should challenge Roman Catholics to be concerned about the ambiguity of the word "merit" in Western Catholic theology. The fact that Luther's concept of *simul justus et peccator*, which shows deep pastoral insight, does not immediately follow from the Pauline argument should caution Lutherans against making it the doctrinal shibboleth for the correct understanding of the doctrine of justification. Methodists will have to examine how a doctrine of Christian perfection or entire sanctification has to be shaped so as not to contradict the message of justification, and Reformed theology may have to consider how some forms of the doctrine of predestination can be reconciled with Paul's insistence on justification by faith alone.

4. Perspectives

Such an integral view of the biblical message of justification will give us also a broader perspective on our present understanding of human misery and God's salvation. It is not only about sin and forgiveness, but also about the breakdown of self-esteem and the acceptance and approval by God's grace. It is not only about me and my God; it is also about a suffering community and the healing and reconciling power of God's righteousness. It is not only about the human soul and the eternal God, but also about a creation groaning and yearning for redemption and a God whose spirit works in the midst of such suffering and "intercedes with sighs too deep for words" (Rom 8:26).

This implies new challenges for our joint efforts as churches to live and to proclaim the gospel of Jesus Christ under the guidance of the doctrine of justification.

What does this mean for our mission?

If God, the Father of our Lord Jesus Christ, is not only the God of the Jews, then he is also not only the God of the Christians but also the God of the Muslims, the Hindus, the Buddhists, and even the atheists—nay, indeed, of the whole of creation. For Paul this insight did not mean the end of his mission but the horizon against which he felt called as a "debtor to Greeks and to barbarians." The gospel belongs to all; how can we share it with everybody so that they discover that it is what they need? The doctrine of justification embraces two different aspects of the great truth that God "desires everyone to be saved" (1 Tim 2:4). It emphasizes God's unconditional grace, which through Christ's "act of righteousness, leads to justification and life for all" (Rom 5:18). And it calls for faith, because God "through the redemption that is in Christ Jesus...justifies the one who has faith in Jesus" (Rom 3:24, 26). God's "yes" in Jesus Christ is valid for all human beings, and yet it waits for the "yes" of those who have heard it in order to have room within their lives. But to hope that God will finally "be merciful to all" (Rom 11:32) belongs to the essence of the Christian faith in God's unlimited love. Therefore, in our dialogue with people of other faiths, we always may have in mind that God "is not far from each one of us" (Acts 17:27). But it is precisely therefore that God appeals, through us, to all people "to be reconciled to God" (2 Cor 5:20).

What does this mean for our *koinōnia*?

Having solved the problem of our differences regarding the doctrine of justification, can we now deal with the problem of our different understanding of the church and its ministry as if it were a totally different and unrelated matter? Should we not try to recognize that in the common understanding of the gospel, as expressed in the doctrine of justification, we have already found the base for a common understanding of the church, its mission and ministry? To take seriously what a theology of justification may mean not only for individuals but also for churches could help to overcome the ongoing competition between churches. Boasting and self-righteousness may not only endanger the relationship between human beings and God, but also threaten the ministry and the faithfulness of the church. Our common faith in the justifying God is already the basis of real communion. Hence, the fact of their common dependence on God's grace urges the churches to review the remaining differences in light of this reality, and to reconsider the weight they may have.

What does this mean for our analysis of the human condition and God's response to it?

At a first glance, the reality of human beings of today seems to be worlds apart from the attitude of people in the Bible who considered themselves to be guilty before God and sensed their need to be justified by and reconciled to God. How can the message of justification speak to people who no longer seem to ask that question? Have we to change our theological paradigm and proclaim a "health and wealth" gospel in order to speak to the needs of people of today? Having studied the biblical basis of the theology of justification, it is our deep conviction that even in our time the message of justification is of crucial importance for human beings. Although not always popular, it challenges the self-understanding of modern human beings and thereby liberates them from the obsession to have to work out their own lives. The healing power of God's assurance of forgiveness, reconciliation, rehabilitation, and renewal affects people of today at the very core of their existence. The social dimension of the concept of righteousness, its clear denial of any idolization of success, greed, or power and its firm repudiation of any effort to value human beings according to their usefulness will guide us to find new ways to live, teach, and preach the message of justification as the deepest expression of the liberating gospel of God's grace in Jesus Christ.

Notes

I. Introduction

1. The Lutheran World Federation and the Roman Catholic Church, *Joint Declaration on the Doctrine of Justification* (Grand Rapids, MI/Cambridge, U.K.: Eerdmans, 2000).

2. *JDDJ*, 40–41.

3. The *JDDJ* does not "lift the condemnations" of the two churches, as it is often said. Rather, it declares that they, while still remaining in force, do not apply to the other church's doctrine as presented in the document.

4. "Justification by Faith," in *Lutherans and Catholics in Dialogue VII* (Minneapolis: Augsburg Publishing House, 1985).

5. "Lehrverurteilungen—kirchentrennend?" in *Rechtfertigung, Sakramente und Amt im Zeitalter der Reformation und heute, edited by Karl Lehmann and Wolfhart Pannenberg* (Freiburg: Herder; Göttingen: Vandenhoeck & Ruprecht, 1986); Eng. trans. *The Condemnations of the Reformation Era: Do They Still Divide?, edited by Karl Lehmann and Wolfhart Pannenberg* (Minneapolis: Fortress Press, 1990).

6. Report of the Joint Lutheran–Roman Catholic Study Commission on "The Gospel and the Church," 1972 ("Malta Report"), in *Growth in Agreement: Reports and Agreed Statements of Ecumenical Conversations on a World Level, edited by Harding Meyer and Lukas Vischer* (New York/Ramsey, NJ; Paulist Press; Geneva: World Council of Churches, 1984), 174.

7. In *Growth in Agreement II: Reports and Agreed Statements of Ecumenical Conversations on a World Level 1982–1998,* edited by Jeffrey Gros, Harding Meyer, and William G. Rusch (Grand Rapids: Eerdmans; Geneva: World Council of Churches, 2000), 485–565.

8. *JDDJ*, 27–39.

9. Methodist Statement of Association with the *Joint Declaration on the Doctrine of Justification* and "Official Common Statement." The Pontifical Council for Promoting Christian Unity: Information Service No. 122 (2006/ii), 55–58.

10. *JDDJ*, 7.

11. *JDDJ*, 9, n. 10 refers to *"Righteousness" in the New Testament: "Justification" in the United States Lutheran–Roman Catholic Dialogue,* by John Reumann, with responses by Joseph A. Fitzmyer [and] Jerome D. Quinn (Philadelphia: Fortress Press; New York/Ramsey, NJ: Paulist Press, 1982).

12. "Official Common Statement," 3.

13. *Condemnations of the Reformation Era*, 24–28.

14. Ibid., 27.

II. Hermeneutical Aspects

1. *JDDJ,* 13, 14. An intermediate level springs to mind when relating Scripture and traditions, namely, traditions of interpreting Scripture. Once exegetical insights and specific interpretational traditions can be brought into dialogue with each other, then a deepening and broadening of the biblical basis of the doctrine of justification will occur. The use of biblical passages in classic Protestant and Catholic doctrinal statements on justification is to be explicitly discussed and clarified in the light of modern exegetical insights. The problems arising from this endeavor will be presented in the following chapter.

2. *JDDJ,* 43.

III. Traditions of Biblical Interpretation

1. Jaroslav Pelikan and Hartmut Lehmann (eds.), *Luther's Works* (American Edition; 55 vols.; St. Louis: Concordia, 1955–), 34:336–37 [hereafter cited as LW]; J. F. K. Knaake et al. (eds.), *Luthers Werke, Kritische Gesamtausgabe* (57 vols.; Weimar: Böhlau, 1883–), 54:185, line 15–186, line 18 [hereafter cited as WA].

2. Cf. *Magistri Petri Lombardi Parisiensis episcopi Sententiae in IV libris distinctae*(2 vols. in 3; *Spicilegium Bonaventurianum* 4, 5; Grottaferrata: Collegii S. Bonaventurae ad Claras Aquas, 1971–), lib. I, dist. 17, cap. 6, 149, lines 7–12. "...just as the 'righteousness of God' is used in the sense of being made righteous by his gift" (ibid., line 11). This expression is used together with other expressions such as "love of God," "salvation of God," "faith of Christ."

3. Ibid., 149, lines 14–15.

4. Anselm's *Proslogion,* ch. 10, in *St. Anselm's Proslogion* with *A Reply on Behalf of the Fool by Gaunilo* and *The Author's Reply to Gaunilo,* trans. with an introduction and a philosophical commentary by M. J. Charlesworth (Oxford: Clarendon Press, 1965), 131.

5. Anselm, *De veritate,* ch. 12, in *Complete Philosophical and Theological Treatises of Anselm of Canterbury,* trans. Jasper Hopkins and Herbert Richardson (Minneapolis: Arthur J. Banning Press, 2000), 186 (iustitia est rectitudo voluntatis, quae rectitudo propter se servatur).

6. Thomas Aquinas, *Expositio in epistolam ad Romanos,* lectio 6 on ch. 1, in *S. Thomae Aquinatis Doctoris Angelici Super Epistolas S. Pauli Lectura,* cura P. Raphaelis Cai, O.P., vol. 1 (8th rev. ed.; Turin/Rome: Marietti, 1953), 20 (para. 102).

7. Ibid., 21 (para. 109).

8. Council of Trent, "Decree on Justification," ch. 7, in *Decrees of the Ecumenical Councils,* edited by Norman P. Tanner (2 vols.; London: Sheed & Ward; Washington, DC: Georgetown University Press, 1990), 2:673.

9. LW 35:189 (WA 30/II; 637, lines 12–17) ("On Translation: An Open Letter, 1530").

10. LW 35:195–97 (WA 30/II; 641, lines 19–21; 642, 6–15).

11. Origen, *Commentarii in epistulam ad Romanos* 3.9 (*PG* 14:952): Et dicit sufficere solius fidei iustificationem, ita ut credens quis tantummodo iustificetur, etiamsi nihil ab eo operis fuerit expletum.

12. Origen, *Commentarii in epistulam ad Romanos* 4.1 (*PG* 14:961).

13. Thomas Aquinas, *Expositio in epistolam ad Romanos,* lectio 4 on ch. 3; p. 56 (para. 317).

14. Johann Adam Möhler, *Vorlesung zum Römerbrief* (Munich: Wewel, 1990), 110–11 (in the original instead of italics: spaced).
15. "Prefaces to the Epistle of St. Paul to the Romans," in LW 35:370–71; WA DB 7; 11, lines 6–23.
16. Joseph Pohle and Joseph Gummersbach, *Lehrbuch der Dogmatik 2* (Paderborn: Schöningh, 1956), 691.
17. "Preface to the Epistles of St. James and St. Jude (1546)," in LW 35:396; WA DB 7; 385, lines 9–14.
18. Ibid., lines 19–27.
19. Cf. Martin Bucer, *Disputata Ratisbonae, in altero colloquio*, Anno XLVI [...] (Basel: Oporinus), 74, quoted in Lothar Vogel, *Das zweite Regensburger Religionsgespräch von 1546: Politik und Theologie zwischen Konsensdruck und Selbstbehauptung* (Quellen und Forschungen zur Reformationsgeschichte 82; Gütersloh: Gütersloher Verlagshaus, 2009), 370 nn. 489–91.
20. Cf. Hauptstaatsarchiv Stuttgart, H 55, Bü. 15, Protocol, part D, referred to in Vogel, *Das zweite Regensburger Religionsgespräch*, 390 n. 577.
21. Cf. Hubert Jedin, *Geschichte des Konzils von Trient II* (Freiburg: Herder 1957), 249.
22. Council of Trent, "Decree on Justification," in Tanner, *Decrees*, 2:675.
23. Tanner, *Decrees*, 2: 674.
24. Quoted from *The Constitution of the Presbyterian Church: Part I, Book of Confessions*, published by the Office of the General Assembly (Louisville, KY, 2004), 80.
25. Cf. Methodius, *De resurrectione* 2.11–8.8; Cyril of Alexandria, *Exposition of the Letter to the Romans* (*PG* 74:809–12). Cf. Karl Hermann Schelkle, *Paulus Lehrer der Väter: Die altkirchliche Auslegung von Römer 1–11* (Düsseldorf: Patmos, 1956), 224–58.
26. Origen, *Commentarii in epistulam ad Romanos* 6.9 (FC 2/3, 274/*PG* 14:1087).
27. Cf. Augustine, *Retractationes* 1.22.2 (CSEL 36:105); *Contra duas epistolas Pelagianorum 1*, 8.22 (CSEL 60:433, 442–43).
28. Thomas Aquinas, *Expositio in epistolam ad Romanos*, lectio 3 of ch. 7, 101–5 (cf. especially 104, para. 576). In the *Summa theologiae* when he quotes Romans 7, he "naturally" sees this chapter speaking of the Christian (STh I/II q. 109, a. 8c and a. 9c).
29. Cf. for example, Pohle and Gummersbach, *Lehrbuch der Dogmatik*, 2:569.
30. WA 56; 341, lines 27–33 (= LW 25:330).
31. LW 31:60 (= Erich Vogelsang [ed.], *Luthers Werke in Auswahl*, V [3rd ed.; Berlin: Walter de Gruyter, 1963], 394, 3 [hereafter cited: BoA V]).
32. LW 31:61–62 (BoA V; 395, 12–24).
33. Gabriel Biel, *Collectorium circa quattuor libros Sententiarum*, edited by Wilfridius Werbeck and Udo Hofmann, vol. 3 (1501; Tübingen: Mohr Siebeck, 1979), 491 (H 26–29).

IV. The Old Testament

1. Citations of early Jewish texts are taken from *The Old Testament Pseudepigrapha*, edited by James H. Charlesworth (2 vols.; Garden City, NY: Doubleday, 1983, 1985).

2. Citations of the Qumran texts are taken from *The Dead Sea Scrolls Study Edition,* edited by Florentino García Martínez and Eibert J. C. Tigchelaar (2 vols; Leiden: Brill, 1997, 1998).

3. "If you do not stand firm in faith, you shall not stand at all."

4. Martínez and Tigchelaar, *Dead Sea Scrolls Study Edition,* 1,17.

5. This alternative is suggested in a footnote in the NRSV, the translation used here for all biblical quotations, unless otherwise indicated.

V. The New Testament

1. Here the *JDDJ* cites "All under One Christ," in Harding Meyer and Lukas Vischer, *Growth in Agreement I* (Geneva: World Council of Churches, 1984), 243.

2. Cf. *Gott angenommen—in Christus verwandelt: Die Rechtfertigungslehre im multilateralen ökumenischen Dialog. Eine Studie des Deutschen Ökumenischen Studienausschusses. Beiheft zur Ökumenischen Rundschau 78,* edited by Uwe Swarat et al. (Frankfurt am Main: Lembeck, 2006).

3. The *JDDJ,* 10, briefly hints at this.

4. Following the *JDDJ* and its criticism, the study by the German Ökumenischer Arbeitskreis (*Gerecht und Sünder zugleich? Ökumenische Klärungen, Dialog der Kirchen 11,* edited by Theodor Schneider and Gunther Wenz [Freiburg: Herder, 2001]) continues the discussion.

VI. The Bible and the *JDDJ*—Conclusion

1. "Annex to the Official Common Statement," 3.

Members of the Task Force

Lutheran participants

Prof. Dr. Theodor Dieter, Institute for Ecumenical Research, Strasbourg, France

Rev. Canon Karl P. Donfried, Smith College, Northhampton, MA, USA (2008–2010)

Rev. Dr. Monica Melanchthon, Gurukul Lutheran Theological College, Chennai, India

Prof. Dr. Karl-Wilhelm Niebuhr, Friedrich-Schiller-University, Jena, Germany

Methodist participants

Rev. Dr. James Howell, Senior Pastor, Myers Park United Methodist Church, Charlotte, NC, and Adjunct Professor, Duke Divinity School, Durham, NC, USA

Bishop emeritus Dr Walter Klaiber, Tübingen, Germany—Chair

Reformed participants

Prof. Dr. Walter Brueggemann, Cincinnati, OH, USA (2008)

Rev. Dr. Priscille Djomhoué, Protestant University of Central Africa, Yaoundé, Cameroon

Rev. Prof. W. Eugene March, Louisville Presbyterian Theological Seminary, Louisville, KY, USA (2010–2011)

Catholic participants

† Rev. Dr. Lawrence Boadt, Paulist Press, Mahwah, NJ, USA

Rev. Prof. Dr. Raymond F. Collins, Brown University, Providence, RI, USA

Prof. Dr. Eva-Maria Faber, Theological Seminary, Chur, Switzerland

Prof. Dr. Thomas Söding, Catholic Faculty of the Ruhr University, Bochum, Germany

Co-secretaries

Prof. Dr. Kathryn Johnson, The Lutheran World Federation, Geneva, Switzerland

Msgr. Dr. Matthias Türk, Pontifical Council for Promoting Christian Unity, Vatican

Scripture Index

Old Testament

Genesis
- 3:5 — 66
- 12–25 — 41
- 12 — 84
- 12:1–3 — 41, 53
- 15 — 40, 41, 54, 84
- 15:1–23 — 53
- 15:1–21 — 41
- 15:1–15 — 41
- 15:1–6 — 41
- 15:1 — 53
- 15:2–3 — 53
- 15:4–5 — 53
- 15:6 — 20, 32, 40, 53–54, 68, 71, 81, 84
- 15:7–17 — 41
- 15:18–21 — 41
- 15:18 — 41
- 17 — 41, 54, 84
- 18:16–33 — 41
- 18:19 — 41
- 18:25 — 41
- 22 — 41, 53, 84
- 38:26 — 36, 40

Exodus
- 1–24 — 41
- 3 — 41
- 3:1–15 — 41
- 6 — 41
- 15:13 — 34
- 15:26 — 35
- 16–18 — 41
- 19–24 — 41
- 19 — 41
- 19:5 — 41
- 20:6 — 34
- 20:17 — 66, 76
- 21 — 32
- 21:1 — 32
- 23:32 — 41
- 24 — 41, 92
- 24:7 — 41
- 34:6 — 34
- 34:7 — 34

Leviticus
- 6:1–7 — 46
- 17–18 — 66
- 18:5 — 79
- 19:9–10 — 47
- 19:15 — 33
- 19:18 — 81
- 24:22 — 33

Numbers
- 11–20 — 41
- 14:18 — 34
- 15:16 — 33

Deuteronomy
- 1:17 — 33
- 4:1 — 32, 33
- 5:1 — 32
- 5:10 — 34
- 5:21 — 66, 76
- 6:4–5 — 68
- 6:5 — 23
- 6:18 — 35

Deuteronony (continued)
6:20	33
6:25	32
7:9	34
7:12	34
9:5	35
12:25	35
13:18	35
16:19	33
21:9	35
27:26	78
30:15–20	78
32:4	28, 33, 36
32:5	29
32:20	32
32:35	71

Joshua
9:25	35

Judges
1:24	34
4:5	33, 37
5:11	31
11:27	42
17:6	35
21:25	35

1 Samuel
2:17	38
8:3	33, 37
12:7	31
12:23	35
15:6	34
18:20	35
18:26	35
20:8	34
20:14	34
26:23	32
30:25	32

2 Samuel
2:5	34
3:8	34
7:15	34
9:1	34
9:7	34
10:2	34
15:2–6	33
16:17	34

1 Kings
2:7	34
3:6	36
8:23	34
11:33	35
14:8	35

2 Kings
10:15	35

Job
	39
9:2	39
9:15	39
12:4	39
16:19–21	39
17:9	39
19:25–26	39
27:5	39
29:14	39
32:1–2	37

Psalms
1:1	101
7:6–11	42
9:7–8	42
11:7	17
17:2	42
24:5	36
26:1–3	42
28:3–4	42
31:1	37
33:4–6	29
35:23–24	37
35:24	31
36:5–6	29
37:5–6	36
37:5	37

40:9–10	31		Ecclesiastes	
40:10–11	37		7:16	36
45:8	31		7:20	37
51	43, 46			
51:3–14	37		Isaiah	88
51:5	37		1:17	33
65:5–13	30		1:27	33
65:6	31		5:23	33
71:2	31		7	44
72	38		7:9	53, 55
72:1–4	30		7:14	9
72:16	30		8:14	55
85:9–13	30		9	44, 53
85:10–11	43		9:6	32, 44
88:11–12	31		11	44
93–99	88		11:4–9	32
97:6	29		11:4–5	38, 44
98:2–3	30		16:5	32, 46
98:9	42		28	55
103:6	32		28:7–15	55
106:31	32		28:16	53, 55–56, 68
118:22	56		28:17	55
130:3	37		35:4–7	90
143:1–12	30		40–66	88
143:1–2	37		40–55	45
143:2	69		41:2	45
145:7–9	30		41:10	45
146:5–7	30		41:26	45
146:7–8	90		42:6	45
			43:1–4	91
Proverbs			43:9	45
3:3	46		43:15	45
10:2	38		44:6	45
11:4	39		45:8	31, 33
11:18	39		45:19	45
12:15	36, 40		45:21–22	45
14:22	46		45:21	45
14:34	39		45:23	45
16:6	46		48:18	45
16:8	39		51:5–7	31
20:28	46		51:5	45
21:3	39		51:6	45
31:9	31		51:8	45
			52:12–53:13	45

Isaiah (continued)

53:11	45
53:12	91, 92
54:17	32, 45
56:1	42
58:2–14	33
58:8	45
61:1–2	90
61:1	88
63:1	31

Jeremiah

3:1	34
4:1	34
5:3–5	34
22:3	34
22:13–16	38
23:5–6	38
23:6	31
23:21	38
33:16	31

Ezekiel

14:14	34
16:51	34
18:5–9	34
18:14–17	34
18:20	34
37	43

Daniel

	51
9:5–18	43
9:16–18	51
9:18	40

Hosea

2:18–22	39
2:19–20	44
2:20–25	32
4:1	34
6:6	34, 44
10:4	33
10:11–15	33
11	43

11:8–9	9
12:7–8	33

Amos

2:6	33
5:7	33
5:11	33
5:21–24	44
5:24	44
6:12	33

Micah

6:8	44
6:11–12	33

Habakkuk

1:12–17	55
2:1–5	45
2:1–4	55
2:4	32, 34, 45, 53, 54–55, 68
2:5–20	55

Zephaniah

2:3	34, 45

Zechariah

8:7–8	46
9:9	31, 46

New Testament

Matthew	92–98, 100–101, 103, 105
1:22–24	9
3:2	93
3:15	12, 94, 98
4:17	88, 93
4:21	92
4:23	93
5:3	96
5:6	12, 96, 98, 105
5:10	12
5:17–20	95

Scripture Index

5:17–19	95	13:19	93
5:17	82, 94	13:37–43	94
5:18	23	13:41–43	94
5:19	95	13:42	94
5:20	12, 93, 94, 95	13:43	94
5:21–48	95	13:49–50	94
5:21–22	95	15:1–9	97
5:21	95	15:10–20	97
5:22	95	15:21–28	97
5:27	95	15:28	90
5:28	95	18:1–5	95
5:31	95	18:3	94
5:32	95	18:6	94
5:33	95	18:23–35	94
5:38	95	18:34–35	94
5:39	95	20:1–16	97
5:43	95	20:16	94
5:44–45	97	20:28	105
5:44	95	21:32	94
5:48	95, 96, 97	21:42	56
6:1–5	96	22:11–14	94
6:1	96	22:37–40	96
6:12	94	23:3	96
6:15	94	24:14	93
6:16	96	25:12–13	94
6:33	12, 96, 105	25:29–30	94
7:1–5	96	25:31–46	94
7:12	94	25:34	93, 94
7:21–23	94	25:46	94
7:21	94	28:18–20	9
8:1–4	97	28:18	93
8:5–13	97	28:20	93, 94
8:10	90		
9:10–11	97	Mark	87–88, 91–92, 106
9:13	97		
9:22	91	1:15	88
9:35	92, 93	2:1–12	90
10:7	93	2:5	90
11:4–5	90	2:17	89
11:5	88	5:34	90, 91
11:19	97	5:36	91
12:1–8	97	6:5–6	90
12:28	92	9:24	90
13	93	10:14	88

Mark (continued)	
10:45	91, 105
10:52	91
12:10	56
12:30	23
14:22–24	92

Luke	
4:18–19	88
6:20	88
7:21–22	90
7:22	88
7:36–50	18, 89
7:50	91
8:48	91
8:50	91
11:15	89
11:20	89
15:2	89
15:11–36	89
17:19	91
18:9–14	89, 105
18:9	89
18:14	89
18:42	91
19:10	89
20:17	56
23:42–43	18

John	98–101, 105
1:12–13	19
1:12	100
1:16	100
3:3	100
3:5	100
3:6	100
3:14–17	101
3:15	99
3:16–17	99
3:16	99, 100, 105
3:18–19	101
3:34	99
3:35	99
3:36	99
4:7–15	100
4:10	100
4:14	99
4:36	99
5:24	99
5:26	100
5:39	99
6:22	100
6:27	99, 100
6:37	99
6:40	99
6:44	99
6:47	99
6:50	100
6:51	100
6:54	99, 100
6:56	100
6:57	100
6:63	99
6:65	99
6:68	99
7:39	99
7:53–8:11	89
8:24	99
9:41	99
10:17	99
10:28	99
11:25–26	100
12:25	99
12:46	99
12:50	99
13:1	34, 99
13:3	99
13:34	99
14:10–11	100
14:16–17	99
14:21	101
15:1–17	100
15:1	100
15:4	100
15:5	100
15:6	100
15:9	99
15:12	99

Scripture Index 125

15:17	99	3:9	114
15:27	20	3:11	53
16:7–11	98	3:21–31	59
16:8–9	99	3:21–26	68, 71
16:11	101	3:21	81, 91
16:23	100	3:22	83
17:2	99	3:24–28	20
17:3	99	3:24	72, 73, 111
17:24	99	3:26	111
17:26	99	3:27–31	68, 81
20:31	100	3:28	18, 19, 68–69, 83
Acts	87, 105	3:30	83
2:33	9	3:31	81
4:11	56	4	78, 84
10	87	4:1–8	18
13:38–39	87	4:1	114
15	11, 66	4:2–22	19
15:5	66	4:2–5	85
15:9–10	87	4:2	81
15:19–20	66	4:3	53, 68, 71
15:28–29	66	4:4	72
17:27	111	4:5	69
		4:6	20, 69
Romans	11, 15, 17, 19–20, 63, 77, 84, 86, 87, 115	4:9	53, 68, 71
		4:13	69
		4:16	69, 72
1–11	115	4:17	54, 82
1	114	4:19–22	82
1:7	83	4:22	68, 71
1:8–17	66	4:23–24	69, 73
1:16–17	68, 71	4:24	83
1:17	15, 16, 17, 27, 53, 54, 59, 68, 88, 91	4:25	18
		5	64, 84
		5:1–11	61, 73
1:18–3:20	68, 71	5:5–10	105
1:18	17, 71	5:5	74
1:24	76	5:6	73
2	66, 71	5:12–21	62, 66, 72, 75, 83
2:5–16	71		
2:17–29	79	5:18	111
2:23–28	81	5:20	79
3	114	5:21	79
3:1–20	78	6	84

Romans (continued)

6:1	75	9:12	69, 85
6:1–14	75	9:22–24	10
6:1–11	64, 74	9:30–31	69
6:3–4	73	9:32	69, 85
6:4–5	80	9:33	53, 55, 56, 68
6:6	73	10:2	56
6:8	73, 83	10:3	17, 69
6:9	115	10:5–6	69
6:10	76, 83	10:5	79
6:11–14	75	10:8–13	83
6:11	73, 83	10:9–10	82
6:13–14	75	10:10	69
6:13	73	10:11	53, 56, 68
6:15	75	11:6	72, 85
6:22	75	11:16	69
6:19	75	11:26	61, 71
6:23	75, 79	11:29	71
7	21–24, 76, 80, 115	11:32	111
		12:19	71
7:1–12	80	13:8–9	81
7:1–6	72, 75	13:9	76
7:7–25	80	14:10–12	71
7:7–24	75	15:8	71, 82
7:7–12	80	15:14–19	66
7:7	66, 76		
7:11	80	1 Corinthians	63–64
7:12	78	1–2	64
7:14–25	21	1:8–24	63
7:14	80	1:9	71
7:15–20	80	1:29	81
7:15–16	22	1:30	63, 75
7:24	65, 80	1:31	81
8:1–2	71, 73	3:9	73
8:6	74	3:12–15	71
8:11–12	73	3:21	81
8:15	74, 85	4	64
8:20–28	76	4:4–5	71
8:26	111	5:4	73
8:28–31	71	6:11	63, 75
8:31–39	73, 105	8:6	9
8:39	73	9:20–21	64
9–11	69, 71	10:13	71
9:7	73	10:16–17	67

Scripture Index 127

12:3	83	2:16	83, 104
12:12–13	66	2:17	73, 75
12:13–27	74	2:19–20	73, 75, 80
15	64	2:20	83
15:1–11	11	2:21	72
15:3–5	91	3	64, 78
15:8–9	10	3:1–18	69
15:10	73	3:6	53, 68, 71
15:11	11	3:10	78
15:20–28	80	3:11	53, 68
15:56	64, 79	3:12	79
		3:13–14	69, 74, 79
2 Corinthians	64	3:19–25	69, 79
1:18	71	3:26–4:7	74
1:20	56, 82	3:26–28	73, 74
3–4	64	3:26	74
3:12	79	3:27–28	74
4:4–6	64	4:6	74, 76, 85
5:10	71	5	76
5:11–21	64	5:1	74
5:17–21	74	5:3	74
5:17	72	5:5	76
5:20	111	5:6	69, 73, 84
5:21	64, 79	5:13	74
6:1	73	5:14	81, 84
10:17	81	5:16–26	80
12:9	81	5:16–25	75–76
		5:16–17	76
Galatians	11, 63, 77, 84, 86, 87	5:16	75
		5:18	76
1:4	74	5:19–23	75
1:6–9	11	5:19–21	76
1:13–16	70	5:22–23	66, 76
1:16	78	5:25	75
2	66	6:15	72, 73
2:1–10	11, 66		
2:4	58, 67, 73	Ephesians	85–86, 105
2:8–9	11	1:3–14	85
2:9	67	2	12
2:11–14	11, 67	2:4–7	86
2:14	67, 69	2:8–9	85
2:15–21	84	2:9	20
2:15–16	67, 69, 104	2:12	85
2:15	58	2:14–17	85
		2:19–20	85

Philippians	63, 86, 87	3:4	86
2:6–11	82, 83	3:5	18, 85, 86
3	81		
3:4–11	70	Hebrews	106
3:4–9	70	10:32–39	53
3:8	83	10:38	53
3:9	69, 83		
3:9–10	70	James	19–20, 54, 101–3, 105–6, 115
3:10–11	83		
3:20	74		
4:7	83	1:1	102
		1:5	101
1 Thessalonians	63	1:7	101
1:10	82	1:12–25	102
2:12	63	1:12	101, 102
4:1–8	63	1:17	101
5:9–10	63, 73	1:18	12, 101, 103
5:24	71	1:20	101
		1:21	101, 102
2 Thessalonians		1:22–25	102
3:3	71	1:22–23	102
		1:22	102
1 Timothy	86	2	20
1:5	86	2:5	101
1:8–11	86	2:13	101
1:8–9	85	2:14–26	102
1:10	86	2:14	20
1:14	86	2:17	20
1:15	86	2:18	102
2:4	111	2:21–24	54
2:15	86	2:21–22	18
4:12	86	2:21	19, 101
4:35	86	2:23	53, 71, 101
6:11	86	2:24–26	20
6:20	86	2:24	19, 20, 101
		2:25	101
2 Timothy	86	2:26	18
1:8–9	86	3:3	102
1:13	86	3:9	101
2:22	86	3:13	102
3:10	86	3:15	101
3:15	86	3:17	101
		3:18	12, 103
Titus	86	4:6	101
2:12	86		

4:8	101		5:11	99
4:9	101		5:13	99
4:10	101		5:20	99
4:12	101			
4:14–15	101		Jude	115
4:15	101			
5:4	101		Revelation	106
5:9	101			
5:14–15	101			
5:19–20	101			

APPENDIX

Early Jewish Literature

1 Peter	106		*Apocalypse of Ezra* (*4 Ezra*)	
2:6–7	56			51
			7:46	52
1 John			7:68	52
1:1–2	76		8:35	52
1:2	99			
1:8	98		*Jubilees*	50
1:9	98		1:15–18	50
1:10	98		1:22–25	51
2:12	99			
2:25	99		Qumran	
2:28–3:10	98		1QS XI 11–15	51
3:1	100		1QH XII 29–37	52
3:5	99		1QpHab 8:1–3	55
3:7	98, 100, 101		4Q 521	90
3:9	100		4QMMT	78
3:15	99		4QMMT 398	51
3:23	99			
3:24	99		Philo	
4:8–16	105		*De virtutibus*	
4:10	99		211–19	54
4:11	99		*De praemiis et poenis*	
4:13	99		27	54
5:11–12	99			

www.ingramcontent.com/pod-product-compliance
Lightning Source LLC
Chambersburg PA
CBHW020805160426
43192CB00006B/451